Goose Hunting:
Doing It The Right Way

By Dennis Hunt

By Dennis Hunt

March 1999

TABLE OF CONTENTS

About the Author 4

Introduction 6

1. Why Is It Getting Harder? 8
   a. Is It the Geese? 8
   b. Is It the Hunter? 14
   c. Getting To the Next Level 16

2. The Nuisance Goose Season 22
   a. Where To Hunt 24
   b. What Is Needed? 26
   c. How To Hunt 29

3. The Regular Season: Canada Geese . . .34
   a. Where To Hunt 37
   b. When To Hunt 39
   c. What Is Needed? 42
   d. How To Hunt 49

4. The Regular Season: Snow Geese 60
   a. Where To Hunt 65
   b. When To Hunt 68
   c. What Is Needed? 70
   d. How To Hunt 76

5. Late Season Snow Geese 84
   a. Where To Hunt 88
   b. When To Hunt 91
   c. What Is Needed? 93
   d. How To Hunt 96

6. Advice About! 100
   a. Weather 100
   b. Concealment 103
   c. Decoys and Decoy Spreads 107
   d. Other Equipment 112
   e. Shooting 115

7. Summary 116

8. Recipes 118

About the Author

Dennis Hunt thinks about and studies geese 365 days a year and he loves what he does. He learns something every day and while he doesn't know it all, he has seen most of it. In 1996/7, he followed and hunted geese from September 1 through March 10. He was out in the field over 1,900 hours watching those damned geese.

Dennis has been hunting geese since 1965 and records all of his hunts. On October 22, 1998, near Bisbee, North Dakota, he shot a young blue goose that was the 10,000th goose he has shot alone or with someone. He was using his old Winchester Model 50 12-gauge shotgun with Federal 2¾ BBB shells. Since 1965, he figures he has fired over 200 cases of Federal shells at crows, upland game and waterfowl and has never had a mis-fire. He attributes that to cleaning his gun after each hunt, keeping the shells warm and dry in the field and using good shells.

Dennis Hunt has written four other books and has produced one video; these are available directly from Dennis or at many sporting goods stores:

1994–*The Science of Snow Goose Hunting*
1995–*Goose Hunting: Improving Your Skills*
1996–*Out-Finessing The Geese*
1997–*The Goose Hunter: The Ultimate Goose Hunting Season*
Video: *The Science of Goose Hunting*

If you want a book/video or just want to talk about goose hunting, be sure to call, fax or write Dennis at:
1265 Loring Avenue #205
Detroit Lakes, MN 56501
Fax and phone: 218-847-5147

If you would like to purchase any of Dennis Hunt's previous books or the video, see page 120 of this book for information.

Contributing Photography: Bill Marchel

Book layout and design: Teresa Marrone

Book Contributors:
George Gage, U.S. Fish and Wildlife Service
Rick Julian, U.S. Fish and Wildlife Service
John Lohman—Fargo, North Dakota, Forum.

Dennis Hunt would like to acknowledge the following companies whose assistance helped make this book possible:

North Wind Decoy Company
        Fergus Falls, Minnesota
Federal Cartridge Company
        Anoka, Minnesota
Higdon Motion Decoy Company
        Metropolis, Illinois
Scheels All Sports Stores
        North Dakota, South Dakota, Iowa, Montana, Minnesota and Wisconsin.

Introduction

After having a total knee transplant on October 13, 1997, and having my goose hunting season wiped out, I am back at it and I am more enthused than ever about killing geese. I have hunted 13 weeks in 1998, and if they extend the snow goose season beyond March 10, I will be out there banging away for another 8 weeks.

The challenge of getting a goose is getting harder and I want to pass on some of my secrets and advice to help you get to the next level. I hunted giant Canada geese during the "nuisance goose season" near Detroit Lakes, Minnesota. I thought I would be going after the stupid giants that live on golf courses and have a 4 handicap, or those clad in a bathing suit living on the city beaches. But in fact, the geese I chased were very wild, and I am going to tell you how to get them.

I also hunted snow, blue and small Canada geese while hunting in Manitoba, and found they can make you humble. I hunt the snows from the Mississippi flyway that come from James Bay and fly through Manitoba, North Dakota, Nebraska and on to Arkansas. These geese have 80% blues in their population and 20% snows, and they are tough as nails because they are chased and hunted hard. I will tell you how you can out-finesse these devils. This book will tell you how to get Canada geese, and how to get the snows during the late season. I'll also give advice about decoys and decoy spreads; concealment; equipment; shooting; and how weather comes into play. I hope this book will improve your skills, get you to the next level and increase your odds against those damned geese.

Why Is It Getting Harder?

A. Is It the Geese?

There are over 1,400,000 geese born each year in North America and 950,000 are harvested. Of the 950,000 killed, most of them are geese that were born that year. The older geese that survive are that much warier and the young that survived got a good education. On March 10 of each year, the regular hunting season closes and the average age of the surviving geese will be:

➤ Canada geese: 6 years
➤ Snow geese from the Mississippi flyway: 11 years
➤ Snow geese from the Central flyway: 8 years

These geese are getting tough to get because they have seen every decoy spread imaginable, they have heard every goose call out there, and they know

These snows and blues are old geese. The average age of a Mississippi flyway snow goose is 11 years.

what the next move of the goose hunter will be. Living a long life is their desire and they don't want to die. They can't be killed by amateur goose hunters with no goose hunting experience who are using less than quality decoys. These geese will only be killed when they are out-smarted by experienced goose hunters using superior equipment and tactics, who are in the right place at the right time and are aided by poor visibility and strong winds.

Geese have a strong survival instinct with super memories. After surviving that first season, the urge to live a long life is very strong and they are not going to commit suicide. Geese were fooled for years by paper plates, white napkins, old tires, homemade silhouette decoys, rags, cheap kites, and improperly concealed hunters. The surviving geese that witnessed their family members and friends die because they were fooled by these methods will not let it happen to them. A goose cannot think or reason because God did not give them that ability, but he sure gave them great memory powers, super eyesight and great hearing.

If you watch geese as many hours as I do and listen to them communicate while they are flying, you will understand what is taking place. They are talking amongst themselves to stay in touch and let each goose know what is happening.

Two of us were hunting snow geese on October 27, 1998 near Belmont, Manitoba. The area can be good at times but the motel and food accommodations at the Belmont Motel are a good reason to be around there. Anyway, we had set up in a barley field that was 320 acres in size. We had 72 Higdon full-body decoys with big feet in white, and 30 Clinton big foots with Canada bodies and white heads. This combination makes a great looking blue goose! We

When snow geese get in a swarm like this, they will be difficult to decoy. But what a sight!

complemented the big foots with 144 North Wind windsocks that had 100 white skirts and 44 Canada skirts with white heads, That also makes a nice looking blue. The spread looked great and we were in Final Approach blinds, probably the best low-profile blind ever invented. We had the 3 elastic tiers that go around the blind loaded with flax straw. We also had lots of long flax straw on top of the blinds, and there was not a goose or mallard that knew we were in the field 30 yards downwind from the decoy spread.

We had harvested 13 snows/blues and 9 mallards, and the action had slowed down on this sunny afternoon. The wind was blowing out of the southwest at 8 mph. We almost fell to sleep when we heard some geese coming from the North. There were 9 of them and all of them were blue geese. They were headed for Rock Lake and were flying 35 mph when they spotted our decoys. They slowed down to 20 mph as they got even with the spread and I was giving them a hail call from one of four differently pitched snow goose calls. They were 100 yards up when 2 young blues and then another 2 young blues dropped out of the flock and slid off to the side. I was clucking on a call and they were getting into position to fly over the decoy spread, when an old blue goose flew from in the middle of the flock and went "awk, awk, awk, awk" at the 4 young blues, who then scrambled to get back into the formation as the 9 blue geese flew towards the lake.

We don't know for sure what the old blue told her kids, but I would guess it was, "Those are decoys, you fools! Get back in formation before you get shot!"

Geese have to communicate in order to survive. You have to let the right wing know what the left wing is going to do.

Fourteen days prior to this, we were also hunting in southern Manitoba. Another event happened that was similar to this one and I would like to tell you about it.

We got to our hunting area and were out scouting when we spotted 8,000 snows and blues. This was the only flock of any significance. There were small flocks of 50 to 100 that weren't worth trying to decoy so we decided to go after the large flock.

They were in a 160 acre barley field and they had started to feed in this field that morning. We knew that because the land owner told us as we asked him for permission. The field had a dried-up drainage ditch that bordered this field and another field to the North that also had barley in it.

We got out to our spot on Monday morning and found that this large flock of Mississippi Flyway geese were super wary and knew what decoys were and would not decoy into this field. Instead, they chose a wheat field, one mile to the East.

We had put out 144 North Winds, 300 Outlaw snow silhouettes, 72 Higdon full-bodies with big feet and 36 Clinton big foots with Canada bodies and white heads. The North Winds had 100 white skirts and 44 Canada skirts and they all had white heads. It was a good looking spread and we put the decoys on the south side of the dried up creek because the wind was blowing out of the South at 25mph. We hid in the tall weeds in the creek and the geese and mallards never knew we were waiting for them.

You could hunt from sunrise to sunset, and at this point it was about 4 pm. We had harvested 10 young snows/blues that morning, along with 11 mallards. All the geese had decoyed in that morning alone or in pairs. We had decided to use the field again that afternoon because we knew we would get some action, even though all the older geese knew there were goose decoys in the field.

We had killed another 4 geese and 6 mallards, when the wind started to blow at 35 mph. We were watching a flock of black geese coming at us and realized they were medium sized Canada geese. They were having a tough time flying against the wind as they flew towards us. There were 36 in the flock and they were 70 yards up as they approached our decoys. We had 36 Outlaw silhouettes in Canada set up off to the side and they might have spotted them.

Wes Kafka, from Bloomington, Minnesota was my hunting partner and he shot at a goose as they were flying over him, low and slow. He dropped the second goose in the flock and the leader let out a "awk, awk, awk" as the flock of Canadas took a 180-degree turn and flew back. They gained another 80 yards of altitude as they flew over us for the second time. This was another interesting scenario of what is taking place in the flock as they are flying.

Geese use the same routes and fly over the same areas about the same time each year. The same goose hunters are using the same fields and have the same decoys and decoy spreads. If you are hunting snow geese in southern Manitoba and are in one of those fields, the geese will know who you are and will be looking for you as they avoid you. These are clever and well educated geese that average 11 years old. They will go thru North Dakota, thru Nebraska and end up in Arkansas. They will be pounded 5 to 10 times per day in North Dakota and won't get any rest until they get to Arkansas because the boys down there will be hunting their mallards. When they leave Arkansas on February 1, they go back thru Nebraska where "the killers" will be waiting for them during the late season snow goose hunt. They will get chased out of Nebraska and go thru South and North Dakota, thru Canada and end up on the Tundra around May 15. They could be shot at 10 times a day during the late season snow goose hunt. Is it any wonder that these Mississippi Flyway geese

This flock of Canadas near Alma, Nebraska knows what the sound of a shotgun is, and have seen their share of decoys.

are wary? Practice makes perfect and these geese get plenty of practice trying to avoid the hunters and their shotguns.

B. Is It the Hunter?

You should have realized how old and clever the geese are after reading the last part. Is the hunter staying with the goose or is he falling behind? Looking at the population increases the giant Canada and the snow/blue geese have made and the answer is obvious. We are losing the battle with the giant Canada geese that live near large cities and losing the war with the snow/blue goose.

You can blame Environment Canada for the decline in medium sized Canada geese. They have allowed Native American Indians to slaughter the geese in the Spring before they have a chance to breed and multiply.

Most goose hunters will hunt 6 to 8 times per hunting season. They will take a week's vacation or

Geese are getting older and more wary. Trying to bag one is becoming more difficult for the hunter, and requires attention to detail.

The average age of a Canada goose is 6 years. They are getting tough to harvest, and the average hunter who puts in just 6 to 8 days per season won't have much success.

hunt 2 or 3 week-ends a season. They have other priorities, i.e. wife, kids, job or other hobbies. They don't take goose hunting serious and they don't make any progress. They don't have meetings to review their mistakes of the past season and don't understand why the geese evaded them. They don't give it a thought that weather might have been a factor when the geese didn't show up. They didn't realize they were putting extra pressure on the geese when they were chasing them near roads, shooting them off their roost, shooting them off roads or sky-busting. Neither did they remember to:

1. Paint their shiny shell decoys.
2. Replace the lost heads on their full-bodies.
3. Put duct tape on their torn wind socks.
4. Test their un-faithful kites.
5. Replace the non-effective bale blind.
6. Invest in any new equipment.
7. Check out their shotgun or inventory their shotgun shells.

Shooting a gun effectively is a mental game. If you are convinced that everything you did in preparation for that day's hunt was right, you will shoot well. If nothing goes right out on the field and turns out broken or won't work correctly, you don't have a chance of shooting well. You will start bitching and think about going home or getting drunk while the geese are flying away unmolested.

The serious goose hunter makes preparations 9 months in advance so he can have a successful goose hunt. There aren't enough serious goose hunters to put a dent in the goose populations.

When you see the skies black with geese and the field below covered with them as in this photo, you'll understand that there aren't enough serious hunters to put a dent in the snow goose populations.

C. Getting To the Next Level

Most goose hunters aren't concerned about getting to the next level of goose hunting. They are happy to get out of town with the gang and have a good time. Getting to be one of the best is for a select few that have the competitiveness raging in them. They want to kill and they want to learn. That is why there are so few excellent goose hunters out there.

Goose hunters born on farms or in small towns are usually good hunters. Those born in Louisiana, Texas, Oklahoma, Iowa, Arkansas, Nebraska, Kansas and Mississippi have the hunting instinct bred into them because their ancestors have been hunting for years. In some of these states, there was nothing else to do.

The goose hunters that grew up in large cities and never spent time on a farm are usually the worst hunters. They often have no hunting instincts or heritage, and it takes them a long time to learn.

During the goose hunting seminars I present, I've met a lot of hunters who need help and instruction. A good seminar can shorten the amount of time it takes to learn the art of goose hunting.

How does a serious goose hunter get to the next level? Through evaluation and the desire to correct faults. Get your hunting team to submit an evaluation sheet and call a team meeting to discuss the answers.

The things to evaluate and discuss are:

1. Is your hunting team organized?

2. Proper timing.

3. Finding places to hunt.

4. Selecting the proper fields in which to set up your decoys.

5. Decoys and decoy placement.

6. Concealment.

7. Triggering the geese to get within range.

8. Equipment.

Let's talk about each item so you can have a meaningful discussion with your hunting team.

An organized team with good, hard-working hunters, spells the difference between success and failure. Gordy Steinwig from Brooklyn Park, MN and Scott Hanson from Buffalo, MN have only been hunting geese for two years, but are good hunters, with the desire to succeed.

1. *Is your hunting team organized?*
   Having a good team captain and lots of meetings is important. Having a 5-minute meeting on the field before each hunt is important. Do you have proper hunters on your team? If you have a heavy drinker or a guy into drugs, it is time to make a change. There is an accident waiting to happen.

2. *Proper timing.*
   Has your team been selecting the right time to hunt those geese? We will go over that later in this book, but this is an important question. Geese that migrate south have been arriving later each year. Hunters that have been going to Devils Lake, North Dakota during the second week of October have found that the geese are arriving November 1st through the 8th, if they show up at all. This is worth discussing. Hunters in southern

Illinois have had to wait until late January to get a shot at a goose.

3. *Finding places to hunt.*

    Are good places to hunt harder to find than they used to be? Are some of your "honey holes" tied up by someone else? This is worth some thought. It might be time to make a deal with the land-owner in your hunting area. There is no "free lunch" any more and all good things come to an end. Paying cash for a lease, or trading some services to the landowners, might be worth some consideration. Outfitters are leasing good hunting lands more and more, and you are going to find yourself S.O.L. some day.

4. *Selecting the proper fields in which to set up your decoys.*

    If this has been a problem for your team, then you should discuss it together. Geese go where they want to go, and if your field isn't one of their

Wes Kafka from Bloomington, MN has gotten to the next level. His decoys are on a good field, and arranged so they look real.

choices, you will be out in the field sleeping instead of shooting.

5. *Decoys and decoy placement.*

    Has your team had a problem getting the geese to give you a good look? If it isn't the field selection, it must be the decoys, decoy placement, or concealment. When was the last time anyone on your team inspected your decoys? All things get old, break or need repair. Shells, full-body decoys, and North Wind windsock heads should all be inspected annually, and some should be spray-painted with flat white or black paint to take away the shine.

6. *Concealment.*

    This has probably been your biggest problem. We will talk about this subject at length later in the book, however, you can't talk about this subject enough. You have to have a good place to hide, and you need some

Some hunters don't have a clue about concealment! A high-profile blind like this won't work on that wide-open field.

advice. There are lots of blinds for sale in hunting publications, and many of these are worthless. I have tried them all, made a lot of them, and finally found one I am satisfied with; I'll tell you about it in the Concealment chapter.

7. *Triggering the geese to get within range.*

    If this has been a problem for your team, you had better discuss it. Over-calling or over-flagging can scare geese away instead of getting them within range. Of all the goose-call owners out there, only 2% are qualified to use their call. Are you or one of your hunting buddies in that remaining 98% of poor goose callers? This is worth talking about, and making a decision on what to do with the calls. The team captain should be the one to make that decision.

8. *Equipment.*

The goose hunting team members should look over your list each year and decide what new equipment is needed. Each guy should be prepared to throw in $100.00 annually to upgrade any decoys, blinds or camouflage, or make any needed repairs to your equipment. It gets frustrating when you are missing something, or an item breaks in the field and needs repair.

Preparations are important to serious goose hunters. You have to have your crap together if you are going to kill a goose. Being lucky won't help.

Getting it all together and using the basics will get results. The author got his share while hunting in Manitoba.

The Nuisance Goose Season

Back in the 1960's, everyone thought the giant Canada goose was extinct. A few years later the goose was discovered at Silver Lake within the city limits of Rochester, Minnesota. That was a wonderful story and was the beginning of the "nuisance goose hunting seasons" held in most Northern states. Since those days, the giant goose populations have gotten out of hand in Rochester and lots of these magnificent birds have been re-located to other states; at this time, their populations are out of control.

When birds or animals get over-populated, problems surface. Crops of farmers are eaten up, city beaches and golf courses are littered with goose droppings and airplane safety near airports decreases. What happens then? State Department of Natural Resources telephones start ringing from complaints about the big geese. So what has happened as a

These geese don't look like a nuisance, but they are. They live near golf courses and airports, and on city beaches.

result of the ringing phones and all the complaints? A "nuisance goose hunting season" now takes place in most northern states and this cre-ates a lot of monies for: licenses, shells,

This beautiful Canada goose is your target during the nuisance goose season.

guns, clothing, motels, food, gas and for farmer's land to lease. It doesn't solve the population of the giant Canada goose but, it takes the pressure off the State DNR phones.

When do you hunt the giant geese that weigh between 10 and 15 pounds? Some are heavier and that depends on what liar is bragging about his harvest. Regulations are set up by individual states and they announce their nuisance goose hunting seasons and bag limits. In Minnesota, the season in 1998 was September 5 thru September 15 and December 11 thru 20. Most of the state was open for the September hunt and parts of the state for the December hunt. Minnesota has limited success the first two days of the special season. After that, the surviving geese are educated and stay within the city limits where there is no hunting or they might migrate to a wildlife refuge. Some of these giant city geese never hear the roar of a shotgun because they are born in a large city and stay there until they die. There is no reason for these geese to migrate because there is open water all year, plenty to eat and no hunting pressure.

A. Where to Hunt Nuisance Geese.

This problem exists in all states because the "nuisance goose season" interests a lot of goose hunters. Most of the states have this special season 30 days before their regular goose hunting season. With the exception of West Virginia, this is the only season for goose hunters on the east coast.

Because of the generous limits offered by individual states and the fact most hunters haven't fired a gun for 10 months, everybody wants to go goose hunting. THE RESULT? Supply and demand comes into play and there is a huge demand to find land on which to kill a goose and a shortage of land on which to hunt. The land you want to hunt on has to have

Finding good agricultural land in which to set up decoys and hunt could be difficult. Look for farm land with fields like this.

harvested crops that might attract a goose. Anything less than that won't work. So already we have a huge problem. The agricultural land, called farms, is owned by individuals who might also like to hunt geese. If they don't hunt, some of their relatives do and they have already asked that guy for permission to hunt his land. This is the scenario you face during this special goose season and it leaves few spots open. If an Outfitter hasn't already gotten to these farmers and signed a lease to tie up his properties, you still have a chance—slim and none, and slim just left the room.

What do you do? You have the urge to kill a goose and must have a place to hunt. You play the game, "Let's make a deal."

1. You go knock on doors and pray that you find a farmer that hasn't made a commitment to his property and feels sorry for you.
2. You lease some land from some farmer and pay $10.00 per acre or more.
3. Find some farmer's daughter and marry her.
4. Try to locate some state or federal lands that allow goose hunting during this special goose season.
5. Get hired out by an Outfitter and hope he doesn't charge you more than $150.00 per day to take you out with 6 to 10 other hunters.

CAUTION! If you find some land to lease, before you sign the lease, make sure he will have some harvested crops to hunt over. Otherwise, you will be "pass shooting" at the geese as they fly over your head.

Lots of luck if you are going to hunt like this! It worked for Girard Faith in 1997 when a brain-dead goose flew over and Girard got it. In 1998, Girard and his daughter, Amanda, were skunked.

2. What Is Needed to Hunt Nuisance Geese?

After you have secured your place to hunt, you are off to a good start. I am going to give you some advice on how to hunt that property for two situations: with, or without, decoys.

Before we get to that and you have decided to hunt for sure, read the "nuisance goose hunt" rules and regulations to decide what state license and stamp/s you will need. You will need a Federal waterfowl stamp and you can start from there. After you get your rules and regulations, read them over a couple of times to make sure you know what you can do and can't do.

HUNTING WITHOUT DECOYS.

Scout this property and watch the geese to know how many are in the area and how many are using this property. Do this daily 3 days before and up to the day you will hunt. You want to know:

To hunt the nuisance goose season, you need a good field, a good spread of decoys, and Eliminator blinds to hide in. We got our limit on opening day with the setup above.

1. How many geese are in the area?
2. Where are they are roosting at night?
3. How many geese are coming into your property to feed?
4. Which way are they coming from?
5. What time are they getting there in the morning?
6. What time are they leaving the property in the morning?
7. What time are they getting there in the afternoon?
8. What time are they leaving in the afternoon?
9. What field are they landing in and what are they eating?
10. Is there water on the property?

With answers to all these questions, you have established a good game plan. If you are going to win the battle or war with the geese, you better have a good game plan.

Equipment you will need:
- 10 gauge or 12 gauge shotgun with Federal BBB shells.
- Camouflage hunting outfit with camo hat.
- Brown face mask or camo face paint.
- Sun glasses.
- Any coffee, water or soft drink you will want.

You are ready for your nuisance goose hunt. Set your alarm clock and get there early. I will tell you how to hunt in the next few pages.

WHAT YOU WILL NEED IF USING DECOYS.

In addition to what you read above about hunting without decoys, you will need:

1. 24 Flambeau shell or 24 Higdon stackable full body decoys. You could use Higdon full body with big feet or Clinton Big Foots. Whatever selection you make, it is a good one.

A good field with a spread of Outlaw silhouette decoys that look good in this picture. Hiding in the corn field would be a natural if the wind is right.

2. 12 North Wind standard windsocks.

3. 6 North Wind hovering decoys. You are hunting geese that might not have heard the roar of a shotgun before. Some of them have never seen decoys before or have never seen a hunter before. The simple spread of decoys with the movement in the spread should bring the geese over your hiding spot and towards your decoys.

Inspect all your decoys and search for any parts that shine. Spray with flat black paint to dull that spot. Decide what decoy spread you will use and I will tell you how to hunt them.

C. How To Hunt Nuisance Geese.
HUNTING NUISANCE GEESE WITHOUT DECOYS.

If you are hunting without decoys, you are at a disadvantage, but it can be done and this is how to do it. You should have been watching your hunting field to learn the patterns of the geese. The afternoon before you start hunting, you have to note the spot where the geese last fed. Knowing that is crucial because that is where you will focus your spot of concealment.

With this homework done and with a game plan in place, you are ready for the geese. You have your alarm clock set because you have to be at your field 2 hours before legal shooting time. You have your hunting team selected with 3 or less companions. Don't take more than that because too many hunters in the field will multiply your problems and decrease your odds against the geese. Remember: an effective small team will bring you results. You are going hunting, not to a poker game. You don't need any dogs or goose calls on this day.

Trying to get near these Canada geese in this corn field will be difficult. You need to have a good plan.

When making your game plan, you noted where the geese last fed. You have watched the geese and know from what direction the geese will be coming. Make a mental note of where you think you should be hiding. Doing that will help you get organized.

You are out to your property and you have 2 hours to wait before you can start shooting. Your first step is to unload your gear and park your vehicle. If you can drive your vehicle out on the field to unload, that's great; it will save you some time and a lot of trouble. If the field is undriveable, a plastic sled with your gear in it will help.

You have your gear out on the field and the vehicle parked near the barn. You are now ready to get organized. Here is what you have to do to be effective:

1. Find the wind direction. The wind is important because the geese will land against the wind and this will tell you where you will be hiding.
2. Anticipate the direction you think the geese will be coming from and heading for. Make a mental note of this and talk it over with your hunting team members so everyone is agreeable and understands the plan.
3. Pick out the spot in the field that the geese will head for.
4. Anticipate how many different groups of geese will be flying this morning. This is good information to have.

With this game plan, your next step is to find your hiding spot. You are looking for a spot between where the geese will be heading for and from where they will be flying. You should be looking for any of these features:

- ditch
- swamp
- grove of small trees
- weedy fence line
- rock pile
- farm implement

If any of these spots of concealment is in the line of flight of the geese, that will be your spot. Get your gear in that spot and get ready. This is the day you have been waiting for and you should be able to kill some geese.

Note: If the first flock of geese don't fly over your hiding spot, but fly 200 yards off to the side, pick up your gear and move under that spot of flight.

GOOD LUCK!

HUNTING NUISANCE GEESE WITH DECOYS.

Having read the information about hunting the nuisance geese without decoys, our game plan will be similar. You will have done your scouting and know where the geese last fed yesterday. You have a spot of concealment in mind and you will check the wind direction in the morning and get ready to set your decoys up. You will arrive at your field 3 hours before legal shooting time. You have a great game plan and should get some opportunities and some geese. That is what it is all about.

This is the field that worked for us while the Higdon and Clinton big-foots attracted the geese. It is hard to notice the Eliminator blinds in the middle of the picture, isn't it? The geese didn't notice them, either.

You get to your field on time and drive out and unload your decoys and gear. Your vehicle is parked next to the barn and you find your way back to the field. I use a strobe light attached to a pole out in the middle of my field. The light blinks 70 times per minute and it brings me back. I shut the light off as soon as I return. Our first step is to check the wind direction. We know the direction and we find our

Using Clinton big-foots will attract a lot of geese. Does this photo look good, or does it look excellent?

spot of concealment next. We are looking for that ditch, small swamp, rock pile or a farm implement. A low spot in the field will work too. We get our hiding spot and start setting our decoys up 40 yards beyond our hiding spot. We anticipate the geese flying over us as they head towards the decoys. No one will be within 40 yards of the decoys. In your game plan, you decided to put the decoys in a horseshoe position with the opening facing the wind. The sentry shell or full-body will face the wind. There will be 3 feeder North Wind windsocks and 3 feeder shells or full-bodies feeding 36" apart and facing slightly into the wind. The other family groups of decoys will look the same and be 20 yards apart. The decoys are all set, your gear is in the spot of concealment and you are ready for the geese. We won't use any goose calls and your dog is home with mama. Today is your day to shine! You did your homework, did your scouting and should get some geese.

GOOD LUCK!

The Regular Season: Canada Geese

The Canada goose is the most popular goose to hunt in North America. The size of the medium and giant Canada provide a nice meal for a goose hunter, if he cooks it properly. There are 13 different species of Canada geese flying around and most of them are small Canada geese, each with their own name. The further North the small geese breed, the smaller the goose. Again—supply and demand. There isn't much to eat at the North Pole, so you come up with a small goose that weigh 2 to 3 pounds compared to a nuisance goose that lives in large cities and eats everything fed to them at the city lakes. The giant Canadas might weight 15 pounds or more.

The migrating Canada goose is the third easiest goose to harvest, in back of the nuisance goose and the Whitefront goose. Some of these geese don't get much hunting pressure, so they don't get practice avoiding hunters and shotguns as the snow geese

This is the roosting and loafing area these geese use. Find out where they are flying to and when, then plan to intercept them en route.

The Canada goose weighs 10 pounds, unless you get a giant or lesser Canada goose. Dennis Hunt shows off a medium Canada goose.

Look at those geese in the middle of that field! Get in an area where there are geese and you will get your share.

do. The snows can be hunted 191 days during the hunting season and I have seen them chased 5 to 10 times a day. They get lots of practice flying and they are the hardest to get.

The Canada goose is a grass, small grain, peanut and corn eater. They are in the grass more because grass is usually available to eat. Corn is one of their favorite meals, so check out the corn fields in your hunting location.

Decoying this goose is not difficult. Early in the season, they are very easy but, they get educated quickly and if you change your hunting tactics on them, they can be had.

Let me tell you where I would go if I wanted a Canada goose for dinner. There are 14 different states and 2 provinces of Canada that I am qualified to talk about. I will follow that up with:

➤ When to hunt Canada geese.
➤ What is needed to hunt Canada geese?
➤ How to hunt Canada geese.

A. Where to Hunt Canada Geese.

I will tell you where to go in this section, but I will *not* guarantee you a spot to hunt! The further north you go, the easier it is to get permission to hunt without paying. When you get south of Nebraska or into Illinois, it will get tough. If you hit it lucky and get permission, don't forget to:

- Say thanks.
- Ask to share your harvest with the land owner.
- Invite them to have dinner with you and your hunting party.
- Ask them if they would like a 12 pack.
- Send them a Christmas card and call them to say "hi."

My favorite place to hunt Canada geese in Saskatchewan is Porcupine Plane, in Manitoba it is Oak Hammock near Selkirk and in the United States it is Fergus Falls, Minnesota. Here is my list. I hope I don't offend anyone. I am just trying to help my goose hunting friends.

SASKATCHEWAN—Porcupine Plane and Quill Lake.
MANITOBA—Selkirk and Lundar.
NORTH DAKOTA—Coleharbor and Moffit.
SOUTH DAKOTA—Mission Ridge and Gettysburg.
MINNESOTA—Fergus Falls and Rochester.
NEBRASKA—Funk and Alma.
IOWA—Saylorville and Carroll.
MISSOURI—Sumner and Smithville.
ILLINOIS—Aurora and Fox Lake.
KANSAS—Kirwin and Neosho Rapids.
OKLAHOMA—Butler and Jet.
TEXAS—Rochester and Dalhart.
NEW MEXICO—Las Vegas and Clovis.
COLORADO—Goodrich and Fort Morgan.
MONTANA—Medicine Lake and Nashua.
WISCONSIN—Beaver Dam and Portage.

Missouri, South Dakota and Wisconsin might provide you with the opportunity to harvest more geese for a longer period of time. They have a long season and the geese are always around in large numbers. Wisconsin has Horicon Marsh, that holds 500,000 if it holds one. South Dakota has the Missouri River Canadas and there are always plenty of them. Missouri has the areas near Swan Lake National Wildlife Refuge and Kansas City that provides lots of goose hunting. Foss Lake near the Washita National Wildlife Refuge will hold 70,000 to 110,000 from mid-November thru February 1, but the land is all leased in that area and lots of these magnificent birds stay on the refuge and won't come out. There are great spots in southern Illinois, but

U.S. Fish & Wildlife service personnel are glad to help goose hunters. Above is Darlene Christen at Detroit Lakes, Minnesota wetlands and if you call her, she will tell you if there are geese on their 42,000 acres of wetlands. Darlene, her husband and their 3 sons all hunt geese, and her boss, Rick Julian, is a veteran goose hunter. These people know what they are talking about and can help you when you're planning a hunt.

the geese never show up until late in January when the season is almost over. The area around the Great Plains National Wildlife Refuge near Jet, Oklahoma is a great spot for harvesting small Canada geese. There are 30,000 or more of them in November and December eating in the huge winter wheat fields in the area and land owners will let you go after these birds. The areas near Funk and Alma, Nebraska as well as Kirwin, Kansas hold large numbers of large Canada geese in October through early January. The most impressive spot for small Canada geese is in Haskell County, Texas.

B. When to Hunt Canada Geese.

If you are hoping to get a Canada goose, you certainly have a lot opportunities. The season for non-Canada goose hunters opens in Saskatchewan and Manitoba near the end of September. Nuisance goose hunting season takes place in September or October in most states, and the Canada goose seasons take place as late as February 15 in Texas.

We have the nuisance geese in our areas all year and they are joined by migrating medium size Canadas that will arrive in late September in the Northern states. These are the non-breeding geese that hang around Northern states in the spring and fly North in late May to mid-June to molt. They do this in northern Manitoba with their only obligations being growing new flight feathers. These geese might be 1 to 3 years old and they won't start breeding until they are 4 years old. These are the geese that will tear up the soybean fields in the Midwest and the farmers hate them.

The small Canada geese begin their migration South during September and you will see them migrating thru your area as late as November 1.

They end up eating peanuts or rice in Oklahoma, Texas or New Mexico. Some of these geese might never hear the roar of a shotgun. The giant nuisance geese from the Minneapolis area will hang around the city until they have to leave because the rivers have frozen up. They have the nuisance hunting season in September and December, but the geese won't go out of the city limits to join in that. When they are forced to leave, they will fly southwest to the Lac Qui Parle state refuge that will be closed to hunting for the season. They will stay there until that area freezes up and then fly to Washita National Wildlife Refuge near Butler, Oklahoma where they are

Pictured is a field of 38,000 Canada geese and a small flock of snows at Washita National Refuge near Butler, Oklahoma on November 18, 1998.

almost impossible to harvest. They will depart that area in early February and go home up North without hearing a shotgun or losing a feather to a goose hunter.

I will go over the list of where to hunt again and tell you the best time to be there.

SASKATCHEWAN—The first week in October until November 1.

MANITOBA—Late September until October 25.

NORTH DAKOTA—

Small—October 1 to 20.

Others—October 15 to November 15.

The author is usually in the right place at the right time. Pictured is a young blue goose he shot near Bisbee, North Dakota on October 22, 1998 while hunting for Canadas, snows and blues. This goose was the 10,000th goose that Dennis Hunt has shot alone or with the help of someone else. He has fired over 200 cases of Federal shells (2,000 boxes, or 50,500 rounds) at waterfowl, upland game or crows since 1965 and has never had a misfire. He attributes this to: cleaning his gun after every hunt, keeping the shells clean and dry while out in the field, and using good shells.

SOUTH DAKOTA—October 15 thru December 15.
MINNESOTA—November 1 thru December 1.
NEBRASKA—November 15 thru December 15.
IOWA—November 1 thru December 15.
MISSOURI—November 15 thru January 15.
ILLINOIS—November 15 thru January 1.
KANSAS—November 15 thru January 1.
OKLAHOMA—November 15 thru January 15.
TEXAS—December 1 thru February 15.
NEW MEXICO—November 1 thru December 1.
COLORADO—November 15 thru January 15.
MONTANA—October 15 thru December 1.
WISCONSIN—October 15 thru January 1.

Don't those Higdon Big Foot decoys look good in the background? If you follow Dennis Hunt's list of what is needed to hunt, you can enjoy success like this, too.

C. What is Needed to Hunt Canada Geese?

I've given away my favorite spots and told you when to be there. How many goose hunters would do that? Now I am going to tell you what you need and what you don't need to harvest some Canadas and maybe a few ducks. Ducks are suckers for a good decoy spread and it is a delight to have a flock of mallards or a wave of pintails swarming your goose decoys.

You should compile your own equipment list and check it off before you leave on your goose hunting trip. Avoid being frustrated by looking for something important and not being able to find it because you left it back in your garage or basement. You'll need:

❒ Federal/state stamps and license
❒ Reliable shotgun and backup
❒ Federal BBB shells
❒ Gun cleaning supply kit
❒ Dependable 4x4 truck and any necessary trailer
❒ Tool box/tools, jumper cables and tow chain
❒ First aid kit
❒ Mobile phone and GPS
❒ Strobe light
❒ Flashlight and spare batteries
❒ Plastic sled
❒ Binoculars
❒ Quality decoys, flags and kites
❒ 20-foot pole and pole holder
❒ Hole puncher
❒ Portable blind
❒ Burlap sacks
❒ Brown face mask
❒ Warm hunting outfits/clothes
❒ Sorel boots and rubber boots
❒ Over-the-boot waders
❒ Knife/axe
❒ Camouflage
❒ Alarm clock
❒ Thermos and cooler
❒ Shaving kit

Make copies of this list, and check off each item as you pack it. Let's discuss the items on this list.
• Federal/state stamps and license: Be sure you're legal at all times.
• Reliable shotguns: Check them out before you leave, and make any necessary adjustments.

- Federal BBB shells: This is a good pattern and a great shell. I have fired 200 cases of Federals (50,500 rounds) since 1965 at crows, upland game and waterfowl, and have had *zero misfires*.
- Gun cleaning supply kit: You'll pick up a lot of dirt and mud in the fields, and will need to clean your shotgun nightly to avoid a problem.
- Dependable 4x4 truck and trailer: You will be out in muddy fields. Is your truck up to the job?
- Tool box/tools, jumper cables and tow chain: Remember that muddy field we talked about? If you get stuck out there, or if you have equipment problems, these items will help you a lot.
- First aid kit: Every hunter needs one.
- Mobile phone and GPS: Pay attention to the mobile phone. They're great if you have a problem out in the field, lake or swamp, and may save your life in an emergency situation. The GPS can save you lots of frustration if you can't find your spot . What about that tricky entrance way onto a field? How do you find your way out in a heavy fog or blizzard? I use a Garmin XL 12 with 500 waypoints. It is a great investment, especially if you hunt or fish.
- Strobe light and flashlight: The strobe light is a new toy that Garret Walton from Pensacola, Florida sent me. It is pocket-sized

The Emergency Strobe from MPI Outdoor Safety Products

This Otter plastic sled can help you get your gear out onto the field.

and retails for less than $15.00. It is called the Emergency Strobe, and MPI Outdoor Safety Products in North Andover, MA handles it. I put it on a conduit pole by using duct tape or a bungee cord and turn it on. It blinks 70 times per minute and helps me find my field after I have parked my truck a mile away. Did you ever get turned around and find yourself 3 miles from your field as dawn was breaking, the mallards and geese were buzzing your decoy spread and your lonely hunting companions were looking for you? Don't let this happen to you!

- Flashlight and spare batteries: It's pretty dark at 4 a.m. and you still have to see!
- Plastic sled: I have two styles of these. They are great for pulling your gear out onto the field and also for laying in, especially if the field is muddy.
- Binoculars: This is a must if you hunt waterfowl. Take them with you when out scouting to see where the geese are feeding in that particular field you are going to hunt tomorrow.

A good-looking spread of Clinton Big Foot decoys (319-242-8801), a good field, and the Eliminator Blinds make for a great hunt.

- Quality decoys: This is what I have in my 5x8 enclosed trailer.
    - ✔ 120 Outlaw silhouettes
    - ✔ 48 Higdon full-bodies with big feet
    - ✔ 36 Clinton Big Foots
    - ✔ 48 North Wind windsocks
    - ✔ 12 North Wind hovering
    - ✔ 1 T-Flag
    - ✔ 4 Jackites
    - ✔ 2 Outlaw kites
- 20' pole and pole holder: I use 16' and 20' telescopic poles made by Falcon. I have metal corkscrew holders so that the butt end of the pole sits 12" in the ground.
- Hole puncher: You need one of these when you encounter frozen or hard soil. It eliminates breaking windsock or silhouette stakes. It can also hold up camouflage, strobe lights, kites etc.
- Portable blind: I have tried all the portable blinds, and found one that I have fallen in love with. The Final Approach Eliminator is the perfect blind

Eliminator Blind and Hide-A-Pooch Eliminator Blind (541-476-7562) are great blinds that provide comfort and concealment.

because it is low-profile, has a back rest and keeps you warm and comfortable. The flaps open and close and when closed, your head with a camo hat and brown face mask is the only thing in the open. There are 3 elastic tiers you can fill with straw, corn stalks or weeds to help blend in with your field. You throw the same over the top of the blind and your head is covered. There won't be a goose or duck that knows you are waiting for them in that field. I used to use a back rest and throw straw over me as I was laying 40 yards downwind of the decoys. This works, but isn't comfortable. I have also tried other blinds, especially the bale blind. This an accident waiting to happen. You have to stake down the entire blind or the wind will blow you away. It blew me and my hunting companion down a hill

The bad-news bale blinds. The author had poor luck with these.

with our gear and guns being thrown out. The wind rattles the sides and it will sound like a 4th of July parade. The flaps on the top will shake, rattle and roll and scare the birds away. The cornfield style I tried is also shiny and spooks everything, even the sea gulls. Bad news!

- Burlap sacks: You need these for many purposes, especially for putting straw or corn stalks in.
- Brown face mask: Don't leave home without it.
- Warm hunting outfits/clothes: You may not need everything you bring, but if the temperature drops and you don't have it with you, you'll be sorry!

- Sorel boots: They make a great boot and have lots of styles.
- Over-the-boot waders: These are made from Cordura and slip over your regular boots. You have the comfort of boots and are water proof. For more information, call Hunting Classics (770-574-9661). Retail price is $115.00, and they are worth every penny.

The author in his Hunting Classics over-the-boot waders. They're made of Cordura and they slip right over your regular boots.

- Knife/axe: Needed to clean your geese and ducks.
- Camouflage: You never have enough of this along, so bring more than you think you need.
- Alarm clock: Some hunting camps don't have wake up calls. The motels in Canada never heard of a wake up call. Be sure to set it.
- Thermos and cooler: The thermos will keep your coffee hot for a pick-me-up in the field. The cooler will keep your game cold after you've dressed it. Bring a big cooler, or several smaller ones; might as well plan for success!
- Shaving kit: Present a good face to the locals when you're in the restaurant or coffee shop. This helps dispel the image of slob hunters.

Look this list over and review it 6 months before your season begins. Talk it over with your hunting companions.

D. How to Hunt Canada Geese.

Knowing how to hunt geese doesn't take a smart man. If it did, I would be eliminated. You learn the basics and stay with them You don't have to do anything fancy to fool a bird with a very small brain. Most goose hunters fail to use their imagination and stay with the same system daily. They forget that a goose has a great memory and knows who is in each field, what their decoys look like and what hunting outfits they are wearing. They might even know their names. What you have to do is try to establish an intelligent game plan. If you are hunting the same flock of geese that migrated in a month ago, you have to try different decoy formations, different amounts of decoys, different positions in your field, different styles of decoys etc. You have to be creative! This would be compared to a good gin rummy player

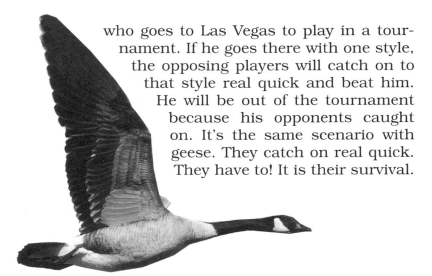

who goes to Las Vegas to play in a tournament. If he goes there with one style, the opposing players will catch on to that style real quick and beat him. He will be out of the tournament because his opponents caught on. It's the same scenario with geese. They catch on real quick. They have to! It is their survival.

To be a successful goose hunter, you must:
1. Be organized.
2. Have good timing.
3. Find good places to hunt.
4. Select the proper fields in which to set up your decoys.
5. Have quality decoys and understand decoy placement.
6. Be a pro at concealment.
7. Know how to trigger the geese to get them in close.
8. Have good equipment.

These 8 basic steps will work on all geese. Of the 8 steps, concealment is the most important. Let me explain these steps one at a time.

BE ORGANIZED. You must have a good hunting team. The team should be hard working, law abiding, and willing to make a lot of sacrifices. No heavy drinkers or anyone into drugs should be on your team. The team must communicate a lot by having meetings to talk things over. There should be a 5 minute safety meeting out on the field before the hunt begins.

PROPER TIMING. You have to be in the area when the geese are there. I told you when they should arrive but, you can't rely exclusively on my word. Always get a second opinion! Call the National Wildlife Refuge or Wetlands Division in that area and get this information from them for the past 20 years. They have that information and will be glad to help. They keep records of when the first goose arrives, when the peak time is and when the last goose leaves their refuge area. You need to know the peak time. They also have weekly bird counts. They take aerial photos of the refuge and can tell you how many geese are in it. Call them a week before you are to arrive to make sure they have geese there. It will be a big confidence booster.

These geese will stay around all winter in some areas. Don't put that shotgun away just yet!

FINDING PLACES TO HUNT. I told you where and when to go and it is up to you to call relatives or friends in that area to get some fields lined up to hunt. If you don't have relatives or friends in that area, someone from your hunting party will have to go there and make some connections with land owners.

SELECTING THE PROPER FIELDS IN WHICH TO SET UP YOUR DECOYS. You have to know the patterns of the geese if you are going to decoy them in close. You have to select a field that they will be going into. To know that, you must:
- Know where the geese are roosting.
- Find out what direction they are flying out to feed each day.
- Know what geese eat and what the flocks you're looking at are feeding on.
- Know where the geese have fed.

You know where the geese fed last and you are ready to go after them tomorrow morning. You have to have a game plan, and you should start by finding the legal shooting time. If it is 7:00 a.m., you have to

Getting a good field is important. You can see that the geese like this field; there are thousands on the ground and more coming in for a snack. This field is particularly good because it has a farm imple-ment you can hide in back of; geese aren't concerned with these.

These Higdon stackable decoys look good, don't they? Lesser numbers of decoys work better than larger numbers later in the season.

program your time so you are finished with the decoys and are in your blinds by 6:30—30 minutes before shooting time. If you have 2 hours of work and a 15-minute drive, you will be in good shape if you are on the road at 4:15. If you get set up too late and the geese and ducks are thinking about coming into your field while you are running to get the job done, you've set the tone for a poor hunt. You want to have time for a cup of coffee in your blind after you have everything set up.

HAVE QUALITY DECOYS AND UNDERSTAND DECOY PLACEMENT. Before you start taking your decoys out and setting them up, you need another game plan:
- What is your objective in setting out decoys?
- What style are we going to use?
- How many are we going to use?
- What formation are we going to use?
- What is the wind direction, and how strong is it?

With all these questions answered, you are ready to go to work. You will find advice about decoy selection and placement later in the book.

Get a good spread out in a good field, and use Eliminator blinds like these. This is a good combination, and it works for Dennis Hunt.

CONCEALMENT. This is the most important factor in harvesting a goose. You will waste the whole day if you are not concealed and the geese see you. You have to realize what great eyesight geese have. If you can see 10 miles on a clear day on a flat surface, the geese might be able to see 30 miles. If you are in a field and move, they will see that movement. That is why I never allow a dog out on the field with us. They might help retrieve a "sailor" but for every goose they get for you, their movement will cost you another 10. I have yet to find the perfect dog to take out to the field with me.

If you under-estimate the importance of concealment, you might as well budget to purchase some chickens to eat when you get home because you won't get any geese. Your best opportunity to kill birds is before the sun comes up and it gets light. That first hour is when you have to make your shots count. After it becomes brighter, it's easier for the geese to see movement or something they don't like, and flare off. Here are some easy-to-remember tips on concealment.

- Use natural cover 40 yards downwind from the decoys.
- Use a ditch, pit, weed patch or a low spot to hide in.
- If there is no natural cover, bring straw or corn stalks out with you.
- Use a low-profile blind and cover it up with straw or weeds.
- **Never lay within the decoy spread.**

I put this in bold so you will really pay attention to this one. The geese are approaching the decoys and they are scared and wary of decoys. They are attracted to decoys like metal to a magnet; however, they have seen family members and friends die because they flew toward the decoys and got shot. They are focused on the decoys because they hate them. Their long necks are out and they are scanning the decoy spread looking for predators, i.e. wolves, coyotes, fox, dogs and hunters that they know will kill them. If you are not in the decoy spread, they will not see you unless you move or talk. They have the vantage point. They are flying 150 yards up and they are looking down. You don't have a chance if you move. They are flying 10 to 20 miles per hour and they are trying to convince themselves that the field with your decoys in has food in it and it is safe. The stomach is telling the brain that it must eat but instinct is telling the brain, BEWARE. If the goose in not convinced that the field is safe, it will not get close. *Remember,* those Canada geese are 6 years old and have seen a lot of decoys and heard a lot of calls and they won't be fooled.

Watch for the farmer spreading manure in the field with this manure truck. The geese know that the manure has waste grain in it, and that's what they're waiting for.

TRIGGERING THE GEESE TO GET THEM CLOSE. You have the geese looking and now you have to trigger them to get close. Don't ever expect the flock of geese to land within your decoy spread so you can kill them all. It will never happen. Be satisfied to get a single, a pair or a family group to break out of the flock and give you an opportunity to shoot your gun. Hunting is a lot of hard work and fun and it revolves around opportunities to shoot your gun. If you select a good field, set your decoys up properly, conceal yourself to be invisible and wait for the geese to get within range, you should get 3 to 5 opportunities each hunting outing. How do you trigger a goose? Do you call and if so, when? Do you use a flag if you know how? You have to know this! 90% of the time, flocks of geese that leave their roost, know where they are going and nothing will change their mind. If they see feeding geese in a field next to your field, you won't have a chance to decoy any geese. There will be a chance later on, when they decide to leave their field to find another field or go get a drink. You could get 1 or 2 to fly over your field. You cannot decoy geese when there are live geese in a nearby field unless you are lucky or there is a goose in the sky that wants to commit suicide. Being able to decide how and when to trigger a goose takes years of experience.

EQUIPMENT. We talked about what you need and we will talk more about equipment later in this book. So now, put yourself into this story and see how it feels.

You have your hunting team, you are in an area where there are geese, you've selected the field where the geese have been feeding and the land owner has given you permission to hunt. You have had a meeting with your team and have established a good game plan. The plan is: Be on the road at 4:15 and at the field at 4:30 a.m. Unload the decoys out on the field, take the personal gear out and park the vehicle. While the driver is parking the truck and trailer next to the barn, the other 3 hunters will be setting up the decoys.

The team decided to use 48 full-bodies and 48 North Wind windsocks and put them out in 16 families of 3 full bodies and 3 windsocks. You'll place a full-body sentry looking into the wind with the other full-bodies and 3 windsocks facing slightly into the wind. The decoys will be 36" apart and the families will be 20 yards apart. The team has decided to put the spread in a half-moon or horseshoe position with the opening facing the wind. The captain of the team noted where the geese were feeding at 5 p.m. last evening, so you know where to start. You found a dried up slough 20 yards from that spot so you will be hiding in there. You set the decoys 40 yards beyond the slough and know the geese will fly over the slough as they head towards the decoys. You've determined the wind direction and

The author is ready for the geese. He is well concealed and the geese won't even know he is there.

knowing that, you know the geese will be going over your heads.

Now you've got the family groups set out and have put 12 North Wind hovering windsocks to the front of the spread. It is 6:15 and you have 45 minutes until legal shooting begins. You've all put your gear in the dried up slough which is 30 yards long by 20 yards wide. Everyone is set to go! It is 6:30 a.m. and time for a short safety meeting. The captain tells you that he will call the shots and he might use his call if he needs to. He indicates he would use the "hail call" only. Your group won't use a flag or kite. You will line up in the slough in a straight line, 5 yards apart. You will shoot straight ahead only. There were no other questions from anyone, so you're back in the slough and waiting for the geese. Now, are you excited? You should be; this is why you are here!

The Regular Season: Snow Geese

The snow goose is my favorite bird, although it has turned me into a humble goose hunter. I have followed, studied and hunted these beautiful birds for 33 years and I love what I do.

Snow geese are divided into 4 flyways, and I'll explain the flyways and the geese from each flyway.

The **Pacific Flyway** is composed of 95% snow geese and 5% blue geese. A black goose is similar to a blue; years ago, a black goose and a snow goose inter-bred and the result was a blue goose. The blue goose's body is brown, grey and black and due to the white genetics, its head is white. The blue goose is mature at 6 years of age, and is called "eagle head" because of this pattern. Anyway, the Pacific Flyway snow geese breed on the western end of the tundra using the Yukon Delta, North Slope and McKenzie Delta. They migrate through Alberta, British Columbia, western Saskatchewan and on to California, western New Mexico and into Mexico.

The **Atlantic Flyway** snow geese are greater snow geese, and these are larger birds. They do not inter-breed and there are no blue geese in their flock unless they picked up a lost blue somewhere along their migrations. These birds breed on the eastern part of the tundra using the Ungava Peninsula and the area east of there. They migrate through the eastern states, stopping as far south as South Carolina. These geese encounter moderate hunting pressure.

The **Central Flyway** is composed of 75% snow and 25% blue in the flocks. Many Ross' geese and

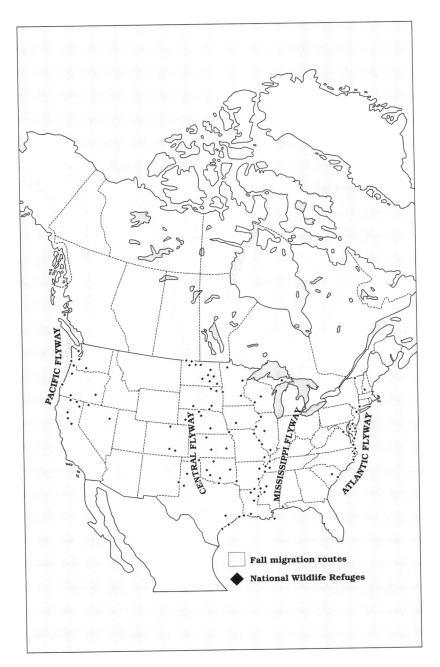

Fall migration routes

◆ National Wildlife Refuges

small Canada geese fly and feed with these geese. They breed on the northern tiers of the tundra and use McKenzie Delta, Bylot Island, Southhampton Island and the McConnell River areas. They migrate down the Hudson Bay south to the Nelson River, west to Saskatchewan and through Saskatchewan, western North Dakota, through South Dakota, Nebraska, and Kansas and into Oklahoma, eastern New Mexico and Texas where they spend the Winter. These geese see very little hunting pressure until they arrive in Texas. They are called "sky carp" in Saskatchewan and are given no respect, nor are they hunted in that area. These geese are easy to kill in Texas because they haven't seen many hunters or heard the roar of their shotguns.

The **Mississippi Flyway** snow geese have 80% blue and 20% snow geese in their flocks. Most of these geese breed on James Bay and southern Hudson Bay. They fly through southern Manitoba where they stage, then go over North and South Dakota, on to Nebraska and end up in Arkansas where they spend the Winter. These geese used to stop in North Dakota but the intense hunting pressure has forced many of them to avoid that state. I have hunted North Dakota many years and watched these geese being chased as many as 10 times a morning. Slob hunters drive through wheat fields with shotguns hanging out the window, trying to shoot a goose as they drive under the flying flocks of geese. That is why a snow goose won't fly over the road while you are driving down the same road. They remember the truck with the shotgun out the window, and won't let it happen to them. Most of these "slob hunters" are from out of state. North Dakota has some very good, legitimate, hard-working goose hunters.

The snow goose is hunted harder than any other goose because it is white and every predator can see and chase it. They figure they will get an easy meal, but *they are wrong!* The season on these birds begins September 1 and lasts through March 10. It is being extended in 1999 and you will be able to hunt these geese until they migrate back to the tundra. With that many days of chasing and hunting, this goose quickly becomes wary. They used to decoy to white napkins, paper plates, rags, old tires and other junk. NO MORE! The Mississippi Flyway snows are almost undecoyable. You can compare

these birds to a mild-tempered dog that is teased with a stick until it growls, snarls, bites and has to be chained and caged. The more a goose is chased, the more cautious it will get. Practice makes perfect! Most snow geese know what decoys are and they hate them. They remember losing family members and friends over the years as they flew towards fake geese and got themselves killed.

While hunting the Mississippi Flyway, I have put out spreads of Higdon or Clinton big foot decoys and complemented the spread with 144 North Wind windsocks. The spread looked alive and very real, with plenty of motion. The field had been harvested and was full of waste barley and/or corn. There were no blinds or other hunters in this field. The flocks of snows would fly over the field and want to drop in for a meal, but they would not; the decoys had put them on alert. Those geese knew what decoys are and avoided this field for three days until I took the decoys out. As soon as the decoys were out of the field, it filled up with snows and blues—road to road. TRUST ME! I tried this experiment on three different occasions in different fields. The point is, these birds are wary, and will spot your decoys and know them for what they are.

The Mississippi Flyway snow geese leave the tundra as family groups and stop their migration at the first agricultural area in Manitoba, between Riverton and Ericksdale. Small grain such as barley is grown there. After eating roots, shoots and berries, they are ready for some real food. They continue their migration southward through Manitoba and get fat on barley, oats, peas, wheat and corn, if they can find it. Their favorite field to feed in is a barley field that was harvested in August and turned over, that has since re-germinated. When the geese arrive, the field has barley seeds and new roots from the barley. This is great for the young geese. The geese continue to build up their group as they migrate to the North Dakota border. There could be over 50,000 in their flock by then, and they will be led by an old blue that is nearly 20 years old. His flock is well-disciplined and won't fly near any decoy spreads. You will kill geese in this flock only if you catch them off guard in bad weather or fog. Hunting snow geese in this situation is a challenge!

If you want to take on the snow goose, let me tell you where, when and how in this chapter.

A. Where to Hunt Snow Geese.

I will give you two spots in 15 states, and two provinces of Canada in which to chase the snows and blues. I have been there, and can tell you that you will be able to get on private property in some of the places. Snow geese aren't a favorite of many people, so you might be fortunate enough to find a good hunting spot. Weyburn is my favorite spot in Saskatchewan, with Belmont and Cypress River being my favorite in Manitoba. Timing is important in Manitoba; the last week in September and the first week in October are the best times. Kenmare,

North Dakota is my favorite place to hunt snow geese in the United States.

SASKATCHEWAN—Weyburn and Rose Valley
MANITOBA—Cypress River and Belmont
NORTH DAKOTA—Kenmare and Tolley
SOUTH DAKOTA—Hecla and Vermillion
NEBRASKA—Blair and Papillion
IOWA—Bartlett and Sloan
MISSOURI—Mound City and Chilicothe
ILLINOIS—Metropolis and Marion
KANSAS—Hartford and Manhattan
OKLAHOMA—Vian and Tishomingo
TEXAS—Garland and El Campo
NEW MEXICO—Elephant Butte and Socorro
COLORADO—Sugar City and Caddou
MONTANA—Medicine Lake and Dagmar
ARKANSAS—Arkansas City and Turrell
MISSISSIPPI—Greenville and Chatham
TENNESSEE—Helena and Ridgely

There are some great spots on this list. Timing is so important, though; you have to be there when the geese are present. The "sleeper states" on this list are Iowa, Nebraska and Missouri. There will be snows in these states until January 1 and sometimes longer. Watch the weather reports and go after these geese. You might find 1 million of them in Missouri in December, and at least that many in Nebraska in late November. The area around Forny Lake and Riverton in Iowa holds 200,000 until mid-December. The areas near Elephant Butte and Socorro in New Mexico provide great snow goose hunting in November and December—this is a "best kept secret." The John Redmond reservoir near Hartford, Kansas provides snow goose hunting well into January. There are always snows there, even in

If you travel in pursuit of geese as much as Dennis Hunt does, you'll see lots of road signs, too! In Manitoba, **Pilot Mound**, **Indian Springs** and **Baldur** are good spots. **Cypress River** is another winner; call Jim Cassels (204-743-2119) for motel reservations. **Belmont** is another good place to hunt and stay in Manitoba; call Fran Laniuk at the Belmont Hotel (204-523-6144). Belmont and Cypress River are near Glenboro; the hotel/motel in Glenboro has some employees who don't like Americans, so you may want to avoid it. **Bisbee** in North Dakota is best from October 25 through November 7.

Clay Center in Nebraska is another good area to hunt snow geese. Work the areas around the Roman Hruska Research Center and you'll find snows, specs, ducks and Canadas.

the worst Winters. Oklahoma is another "sleeper state." There is great hunting around the refuges of Great Salt Plains, Washita, Tishomingo and Sequoyah.

B. When to Hunt Snow Geese.

Having been there and done it, I can tell you that these are your best chances for "show time." Always watch the weather reports and call ahead. Verify that there are snow geese in your hunting area by calling relatives, friends or land owners. If there is a National Wildlife Refuge or a U.S. Fish and Wildlife Service Wetlands in that hunting area, contact them. The refuges take a weekly bird count, and can tell you:

- how many snow geese are in their refuge area
- how many Canada geese are in their refuge area
- how many ducks are in their refuge area

They can give you soil and water conditions of the whole area. These people are great and want to help sportsmen whenever they can. I leave two self-

Stop in or call the De Soto National Wildlife Refuge at Missouri Valley, Iowa (712-642-4121) and find out when the snow geese will be there. Joan Martin works at the Visitor's Center and can help you.

addressed envelopes with some of my friends at various wetlands in North Dakota, and they mail them back to me to tell me how many geese and ducks are in their areas. I am not home much, so this works super. Geese migrate in and out very quickly. In fact, they might stay only a few days, so you have to be an opportunist and strike quickly. Their stay depends on **water supply for roosting and drinking**, the **food supply**, and **hunting pressure**. If they have lots of food and water but also lots of hunting pressure, the geese will quickly move on.

Here are the best times to hunt each area.
SASKATCHEWAN—October 1 thru October 31
MANITOBA—September 25 thru October 9
NORTH DAKOTA—October 28 thru November 7
SOUTH DAKOTA—November 5 thru November 15
NEBRASKA—November 18 thru December 1
ILLINOIS—November 25 thru December 25
IOWA—November 15 thru December 15
KANSAS—November 20 thru December 15

OKLAHOMA—December 1 thru December 31
TEXAS—December 1 thru January 15
NEW MEXICO—November 20 thru December 20
COLORADO—November 1 thru November 30
MONTANA—October 15 thru October 31
ARKANSAS—December 15 thru January 15
MISSISSIPPI—December 15 thru January 15

C. What is Needed to Hunt Snow Geese?

Snow geese are a lot more difficult to decoy than Canadas so you will have to pay attention. Be sure to take movement decoys along, and purchase a Final Approach Eliminator blind or get lots of natural cover camouflage to take with you on the hunting field. Bring all of your tricks with you because you will have to try harder and use different methods daily to trick these "white devils." Most of the geese

Being in the right place at the right time is important, but so is proper decoying. Dennis Hunt (left) and veteran goose hunter Ken Heinisch (right) from Fargo, North Dakota seem to have both parts of the equation right!

A nice flock of snows and blues near Bisbee, North Dakota.

will be over 6 years old, with the average snow in the Mississippi Flyway being 11 years old. You are not hunting fools! You are after geese that have seen every decoy and spread out there, and have heard every goose call known to man. You are in a WORLD SERIES BALL GAME when you try to match wits with snow geese. You won't need to call because these geese won't be suckered in by a goose call or plastic flag. But they can be had, and in the rest of this chapter I will tell you what you will need and how to get them. We are going to concentrate on movement decoys and concealment because these are our "strong suits." We will discuss how to select a field the geese want to be in and how to make sure you are concealed properly, so you will be in a position to "bang them."

To pick the field that the geese will want to be in will take some scouting and some luck. It is hard to find the field that snows will pay any price to get

For snow geese, you need a good field, a good spread, and conceal-ment. These Clinton and Higdon full bodies with big feet look real, and fooled a lot of super-clever geese from the Mississippi Flyway.

into, but it can be done. This situation comes up only when:

- The geese just migrated in and are hungry.
- They are about to leave and are worried about increasing their body fat for the migration.
- There is a shortage of food in the area and the geese are very hungry.

We will find that certain field and be opportunists by striking fast and furious. We will stay concealed so that no bird will ever know we are in that field. Here is what we need:

DECOYS:
- 360 Outlaw silhouettes in snows, or 30 dozen shell decoys.
- 48 Higdon stackable big foots.
- 144 North Wind windsocks (no substitutes!).
- 12 North Wind new style hovering windsocks (see page 75).
- 2 Jackites with 20' telescopic poles and pole holders.

Complement your field of full-bodies with North Wind windsocks. I use the Canada skirt with a white head to make a nice-looking blue goose. The North Wind windsock may be the best decoy ever invented.

- One Higdon Finisher kit:
  - a. battery and cam
  - b. 6 Finishers
- A helium tank of gas, with the following:
  - a. 48 goose-sized white balloons
  - b. 48 goose-sized black balloons

We will use the balloons in case we have a windless day. The balloons should each have a 4-foot piece of kite string, so we can tie them to our full-body decoys.

DECOY ACCESSORIES:
- Final Approach Eliminator blinds.
- Hole puncher, two plastic sleds and some burlap sacks.
- White and army camouflage, and four white sheets.

OTHER ACCESSORIES:
- Strobe light, flash light and binoculars.
- Over-the-boot waders, Sorel leather boots and

rubber boots.
- Warm hunting outfits, white coveralls and white hat.
- White face mask, brown face mask and sunglasses.
- First aid kit, mobile phone and GPS.
- Tool box/tools, jumper cables and tow chain.
- Dependable 4x4 truck with necessary trailer.
- Federal/state stamps and hunting license.
- Good-shooting shotgun and a good back-up gun.
- Federal BBB shells.
- Gun cleaning kit and supplies.
- Alarm clock, thermos, coolers and shaving kit.

I gave you a list on page 43 that was similar to this one, along with explanations for many of the items. But there are some things on the "snow goose hit list" above that are different, and I'll explain them below.

1. Higdon stackable big foots instead of regular big foots. We will have a lot more decoys with us, and these decoys will save a lot of room in the trailer.

2. Higdon Finisher kit. A battery attached to a cam pulls the heads of six full-body decoys with soft heads. A braided fishing line is attached to the heads and the cam pulls the heads up and down. This system could "blow the brains of the geese" and sucker them in.

3. Helium tank of gas with goose-sized balloons in white and black. This is an "ace in the hole" in case of a lack of wind. We need lots of wind to get the geese off their normal patterns. We can't depend on nature to supply the wind we need. If we don't have wind, we will use the gas and the balloons. This is our day and we are going to succeed in getting our share of geese.

4. Final Approach Eliminator Blinds. I talked

The new style of the North Wind hovering windsock. This decoy is 10 times more effective than the goose magnet, and half the price. Trust me! I used the goose magnet for 9 years, and I know. Below is Brenda Jurgens Knutson, CEO of North Wind Decoy Company. Her dad started the company in Devils Lake, North Dakota 20 years ago and this company has been helping hunters harvest geese ever since.

about this blind earlier in this book (see page 47), and it is a great blind. I fooled the snows day after day in 1998 with this blind. This has never happened to me before. Ducks and geese still don't know that my hunting companions and I were waiting for them in those fields. There will never be a substitute blind for Dennis Hunt to use while hunting geese or ducks!

5. I have added **white sheets, hats and face masks** in case we have to deal with snow.

Now we have the good equipment that we need. Our next moves are to get that "right field," have a meeting with our team members and develop a good game plan. We are ready to go after those snow geese.

D. How to Hunt Snow Geese.

You told me you want to challenge the snow geese and we are almost ready to go on our "fantasy snow goose hunt." I told you all of my good spots and when to be there, and what you will need. We have a few things left to do and we will be off on our "fantasy goose hunt."

We decided to meet in the Rainwater Basin of Nebraska southeast of Hastings. It will happen the weekend after Thanksgiving and there should be lots of snow geese in the area. I had been checking the weather reports and watching the weather channel,

Look at all those geese in that pond, and in the air! How are you going to hunt these geese? You need to have a good plan.

and the weather has been super in that area. To get a second opinion, I called George Gage, the manager at De Soto National Wildlife Refuge near the Missouri River between Missouri Valley, Iowa and Blair, Nebraska. George is a 33-year veteran of the U.S. Fish and Wildlife Service and runs the finest facilities at De Soto and Boyer Chute as well as having the most responsibilities. George told me, "De Soto has 650,000

George Gage raises the flag at De Soto National Wildlife Refuge. He has worked for the U.S. Fish and Wildlife Service for 33 years, and really knows his stuff.

snows and the Rainwater has lots of them, too." I made another call to a friend near Ong, Nebraska and he told me, "You had better get here, because they are all over the place." That was good enough for me!

I got to the hunting area one day early to scout the area out, and I liked what I saw. I also found the "right corn field" where I was sure we would get a lot of opportunities to kill some snow geese. The farmer had harvested the field two weeks ago and it was cut down to 2" high, perfect for decoys and my Eliminator blinds. The geese had found the field and began feeding in it yesterday. There was lots of spilled corn in this field because I could see some of it from the roadside. The field was 160 acres, and the land was almost flat with a few ridges and low spots.

The author and his hunting companions harvested these geese and ducks while hunting in Nebraska.

There was no natural cover in the field, so my blinds would be a necessary item. They have cornfield design on them and would blend in perfectly. The farmer was holding the field for us and I was very excited.

Our hunting party met the afternoon before at the motel and I greeted them. I told everyone about "our spot" and we went out to look it over. We would talk things over and develop a good game plan. We looked the field over at 4:00 p.m. and things looked positive. The field was "road to road" with snow geese and a few whitefronts. We watched the geese with binoculars and determined there were 10% young geese in the flock, and that the majority of the geese were blues. We would be hunting geese from the Mississippi Flyway! Decoying would be harder with this group of "eagle heads" but I knew they could be had. We noted where the majority of the geese were feeding and that was where we would start the next morning.

Our next step was to find the entrance to the field. We found it down at the corner; it was a level entrance, and a good one. I marked the entrance on my GPS in case we had fog or poor visibility the next morning. We then left the area and went back to the motel to talk things over.

Legal shooting time was 7:52 a.m. and we decided to leave the motel at 5:30 a.m. to drive the 8 miles to the field. We would be able to drive out to our starting spot, unload the decoys from the trailer and our personal gear from the truck, then park the truck out of the way. We would then set up the decoys and be finished by 7:30.

We were going to use the following decoys:
• 360 Outlaw snow geese silhouettes.
• 144 North Wind windsocks.
• 12 North Wind hovering windsocks.

We decided to use the silhouettes rather than the Higdon stackable full-bodies because they are higher profile and would be more visible in this corn field. I have containers with 40 snow and 32 blue windsocks in them and we would use two of them. We would compliment these decoys with 12 North Wind hovering windsocks. This is a new version of the hovering and was just introduced. It is half as expensive as the goose magnet and twice as effective. After purchasing my North Wind hoverings, I sold my goose magnets for $2.00 a piece to a young hunter. We would set the silhouettes in the middle of our spread with the windsocks surrounding the silhouettes and the hoverings downwind in pairs. The decoy formation would be a half-moon or horseshoe position. The opening would be facing the geese as they would come in against the wind. We would not use any kites. The field was certain to attract geese and we did not want to use anything we didn't need that could "spook" these geese. We would not call or use a flag. We would concentrate on concealment. We had talked things over and we were satisfied we were organized. We retired at 9:00 p.m. and prayed for some winds to give the North Winds some motion in the morning.

We left at 5:30 a.m. and drove to the field. The wind was blowing 12 mph from the northeast. Our prayers were answered! The sky was overcast and luck was with us—cloudy skies and wind. We drove out on the field and found the area where the geese were at 5pm yesterday. That is where we would start. Our first move was to find a location for our 4 Eliminator blinds and we found a low spot 40 yards downwind. We were ready to unload and go to work. The ground was soft and setting the Outlaws up was a piece of cake. We left the head lights on and the visibility was good. We were able to work without any interruptions and we got done at 6:45. When we were finished, we drove around the spread and looked things over. We also looked for anything that

This dried-up swamp was very productive for snow geese because there's lots of natural concealment. There's fog in the air also, which helps the hunter.

You don't need much personal equipment if you're hunting in a dried-up swamp like the one shown on the opposite page.

might have been left in the field and would spook the geese. Everyone agreed—the spread looked great. We got out of the truck again and found corn stalks to cover our blinds and our heads. We made sure we had all of our personnel gear in the blinds and we were ready for those "white devils."

The 160 acre field was a big one and it was full of geese when we left it yesterday. We had our decoys in the area where most of them were feeding and were hoping the geese would come to us. However, we were not positive and you know "Murphy's law." It was time to park the truck and trailer and I used one of my old tricks. We parked the truck/trailer 350 yards down from our decoys in the corn field. This trick worked for me in Manitoba last Fall and I knew it would not "spook the geese." The truck and trailer don't move and the geese don't pay any attention to them. They won't land near them and that is the scenario we wanted. We wanted the geese to come to us. The only thing they would pay attention to is the

decoys. They would watch the decoys and try to determine if they are fakes or real geese. They would have their long necks out and would be scanning the decoys trying to convince themselves the field was safe. They would be looking and looking for sights of real geese or predators within that good looking spread of decoys. The thing we had on our side was:

1. We were 40 yards downwind and covered up with corn stalks.

2. There was nothing within that decoy spread that would "spook the geese." All the silhouettes had been touched up with flat white paint as had all the plastic heads on the North Wind windsocks. The same had been done to the North Wind hovering, even though, they were just purchased. Our decoys looked great.

We were confident as we sat in our blinds and drank some coffee. It was 7:30 am and we had our safety meeting. We were in our Eliminator blinds with our backs to the decoys and the wind. We were 40 yards from the decoys and our blinds had corn stalks stuck in the elastic around the sides of the blind. Corn stalks would also be thrown over the top of the flaps after they had been closed. Our heads would be protruding from the hole in the center with a brown face mask on and some corn stalks over and around the head. There was no way in hell any birds would see us. The blinds were side-by-side 5 yards in between each blind. If geese looked down at us from 150 yards, it would look like a bunch of corn stalks in a corn field. It would not move and the eyes of the goose would be focused on the decoy spread and not "the killers" waiting for them down below.

I won't go into detail about this hunt. You know it worked and I knew it would work. We did our homework! We got a good field, there were lots of geese around, we had good equipment and we were concealed—the most important factor if you are going to get a goose. We killed three mallards at 7:55 am and the geese started to "roll in." They were apprehensive about the decoys but, wanted that field. These old geese were lead by an old blue that was ancient. We got him and his beak and feet were worn and I know he was at least 20 years old. Wave after wave of snows came at our decoys and we shot and shot. We left our dead geese lay in the field and stayed in the blinds where we were never seen by any bird. The steady shooting continued until 10:30 and it was over by 11:30. The geese landed in a soy bean field two miles east of us after we had "hammered them". Others flew back to their roost to get a drink and to regroup. This kind of decoy hunting is rewarding and fun. By the way, the geese never paid attention to my truck/trailer that were parked 350 yards away and in the same field. They might have thought about landing in that part of the field, but would not because of the truck and trailer parked there.

Late Season Snow Geese

Hunting for late season snow geese can be interesting. You don't know what you are going to get—or get into. Weather is an important factor and dictates what is going to happen. Watch the weather channel and make lots of phone calls before you pack your hunting gear into the truck. You might encounter a bad snow storm, ice storm, sleet storm or rain storm. You could have a mixed bag of weather. Driving and hunting conditions won't be normal. You don't know what to bring along because you don't know what you can and can't use. How about the geese you are expecting to kill? I hope you didn't promise any to anyone. This could be unpredictable, to say the least.

The snow geese you will be after are survivors. Most of them are Mississippi Flyway geese who are 11 years old, have avoided decoys and shotguns for all those years and are on their way back to the tundra to breed. And you think you are going to fool and kill these "white devils"? You do have the weather on your side. There will be fast changes in weather and you could luck out.

The late season was a bust in Nebraska in 1996 and 1997. In 1998, it was poor until a blizzard hit on March 6, 1998. Most of the geese flew back to Oklahoma and waited for the ice and snow to melt. There were some geese that were slow to react to bad weather conditions, and some that were too dumb to fly back south. These geese got slaughtered! Hunters killed them without using decoys because these geese didn't know where to fly. They were hungry and couldn't find food. How could they, with a foot of snow on the ground? Some hunters also ended up stranded because they could not drive. Others had

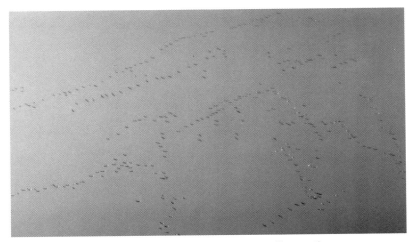

During the late snow goose season, you will see the snow geese 1,000 yards in the air. They will slip wind and funnel down to the fields. This will usually happen in the afternoon.

put snow chains on their truck tires, and many had to be pulled from the ditches with chains.

What is unusual about hunting these snows late in the season is that you are going after geese that will be flying high and from the south. They might be flying against some strong winds and will be tired, hungry and thirsty. If you are in a good corn field with standing water or a body of water nearby, the geese might slip the wind and come down in your field if you have a good decoy spread and are concealed. These geese will be 1,000 yards up and will decoy because they can't fly any farther. You could get lucky!

Most of your shooting will take place in the afternoon. If you are hunting in Nebraska, the geese might be flying from Oklahoma or Arkansas and it will take time for them to get to your area. They are headed for the Rainwater Basin in central Nebraska and won't stay long. They funnel down, eat, drink and rest, and then they move on. You have to be an opportunist and strike fast.

A young blue goose. This bird is three months old and has grey, black and a patch of white on it. When the blue goose is six years old, it will have grey, black and brown on the body with a white head. It never has any blue on it during its life. How can they call it a blue goose?

Selecting your decoys for this season is unusual. You won't know ahead of time if you can drive on the fields, or even down the muddy farm roads. Having some 5-foot plastic sleds along is a good idea. Don't take a big trailer packed with full-bodies because you might not be able to pull the trailer down the road or get the decoys out on the wet and muddy fields. Going "light" would be my suggestion. Take along North Wind windsocks and some stackable decoys. Kites also work well for late-season snows. Get some Jackites or Outlaw kites with a 20-foot telescopic pole and a pole holder.

You must be patient and lawful during this late season snow goose hunt. You might wait until 3:00 p.m. to get your first shot. BEWARE of small Canada geese and whitefronts! They will be everywhere and it is against the law to kill these birds during this snow-goose-only season. There will be many state and Federal Conservation Officers trying to do their jobs. If you are planning to be a "red-neck" or "slob hunter" and break some laws, get a back-up plan in place to get you home. You will have to ride a horse or take a bus if you lose your truck. There will be a lot of hunters during this hunting season that have "hunting withdrawal" and are desperate to kill a goose. These guys might get in your way, so watch it! There is a statement, "a man will pay any amount of money to kill a goose." You will find all sorts of hunters during this late season snow goose hunt.

Let me tell you where, when and how to hunt the late season snow geese.

Pay attention to the law! During the late snow goose season, there are many ways to break the law. Don't be tempted!

A. Where To Hunt Late Season Snow Geese.

This is a hard question to answer. General areas is a lot easier than trying to "pin point" a small town. However, I will tell you where I would try. I have inserted Minnesota, North Dakota, Manitoba and Saskatchewan on this list. At this time, a "conservation hunt" is planned for the states and provinces that will allow hunting until the geese have migrated north. I hope they have those seasons and I am not wrong, because I might be hunting until June 1. Here is my list:

OKLAHOMA—Cherokee and Optima
MISSOURI—Chilicothe and Rockport
KANSAS—Hartford and Leavenworth
IOWA—Bartlett and Riverton
NEBRASKA—Fairbury and Harvard
SOUTH DAKOTA—Elk Point and Houghton
MINNESOTA—Windom and Wheaton
NORTH DAKOTA—Tewaukon and Church's Ferry
MANITOBA—Boissevain and Glenboro
SASKATCHEWAN—Estevan and Big River

The southwest corner of Iowa near Riverton and at Forney Lake near Bartlett are great spots. State areas are available; follow the rules and you will get along fine.

Find a place to hunt around any of these bodies of water during the late snow goose season. Tired geese will be looking for water. You can see how cold it often is during the late snow goose season by looking at the snow in the top photo.

If you are driving around and see white feathers (see arrows in photo) in a pond such as this, don't go any farther! Snow geese are roosting there.

The best spot in Saskatchewan would be Estevan and in Manitoba it would be Boissevain. The best spots in the United States would be Fairbury in Nebraska and Houghton in South Dakota. Houghton usually holds 1,000,000 snows and blues near the Sand Lake National Wildlife Refuge near the end of March. Call them and they will give you weekly bird counts (605-885-6320) if you are going.

If I was going to hunt any one area and was not familiar with that area, I would plan on being mobile and ready to move in any given direction. You have to be where the geese are! Call all the National Wildlife Refuges, U.S. Fish & Wildlife Service Wetlands offices and all state Department of Natural Resources Offices and they will give you daily information. They can give you plenty of good information. Get to know these people because they enjoy helping the sportsmen and women. That is their job.

B. When To Hunt Late Season Snow Geese.

This is another tough question to answer. It is all related to the weather. The snows and blues have the instinct to leave their Winter residences and head north towards their breeding grounds. More daylight will urge them to leave, as will lack of food or the urge to eat more corn. I could tell you when you might expect them, but that might be like an alcoholic telling his wife, "I am going to the bar. I will be back in 10 minutes." The geese are not as predictable as they are in the Fall migrations. I know that these geese never fly past the "snow line" so you can expect them to be in an area where most of the snow has melted and the waters are open for the geese to have a place to roost.

Here are the times when the birds are normally at various areas. I would suggest calling your Federal and state agencies to get bird counts. They will be glad to help you.

OKLAHOMA—February 1 thru March 1
MISSOURI—February 10 thru March 10
KANSAS—February 1 thru March 10
IOWA—February 15 thru March 10
NEBRASKA—February 15 thru March 10
SOUTH DAKOTA—March 1 thru April 15
NORTH DAKOTA—April 10 thru May 10
MINNESOTA—April 15 thru May 1
MANITOBA—April 20 thru May 15
SASKATCHEWAN—April 15 thru May 15

Everything depends on the weather. When El Niño was with us in 1998, there were snow geese in Missouri all Winter, and in southern Iowa in January. There have been snows that have stayed in Nebraska all Winter many times, as well as in Kansas. If there is food and open water with no hunting pressure, there is no reason for them to leave. If their food is corn, there is never a shortage of it unless it is covered with ice and snow. The geese could get tired of eating rice in Texas and Arkansas and leave early. They are very unpredictable. I wish I knew why:

1. They start their Fall migration and when?
2. They start their Spring migration and when?
3. Why do they avoid some of my decoy spreads?
4. Why don't they come back to the same field as predicted?
5. Why do they migrate out of an area in the middle of the night?

These are questions I would like answered by some of these snow geese because they can drive you crazy. A little bird with a small brain that is more clever than a goose hunter who has computers, cell phones, GPS, radar, etc. Life is a bitch!

You will see large flocks like this during the late snow goose season. It's quite a beautiful sight.

C. What Is Needed to Hunt Late Season Snow Geese?

This hunt will be controlled by wet fields, water, mud, ice, cold, wind, snow and rain. It will be a trip that demands you be mobile, work hard and be prepared for anything. Patience will be necessary to hunt these unpredictable geese. You will suffer through cold hands, wet clothes, mud on yourself and everything else, and wounded pride. These white birds will humble you. They are determined to survive the hunting season and they only have 30 days or less to go. They are not going to commit suicide and will not let a goose hunter fool them.

This is not a normal goose hunting trip. Winter is almost over, but it doesn't want to leave. You are thinking 75 degrees but might see 10 below. This is what I would take on a late season snow goose hunt:

DECOYS:
- 360 Outlaw silhouettes
- 288 North Wind windsocks
- 12 North Wind new-style hovering windsocks (page 75)
- 4 Jackites with 20' telescopic poles and pole holders

Go light for the late snow goose season! Plan on using North Wind windsocks instead of large decoys. 10 dozen windsocks will work.

The Gun Rap case is essential to keep your guns dry during the wet late snow goose season.

OTHER:

- Final Approach Eliminator blinds (page 47)
- Two 5-foot plastic sleds (page 45)
- Hole puncher and burlap sacks
- White sheets, white and army camouflage
- Strobe light (page 44), flashlight, camera and binoculars
- Over-the-boot waders (page 48)
- Sorel leather boots and rubber boots
- Warm hunting outfits, snowmobile suit, white coveralls and white stocking hat
- White face mask, brown face mask and sun glasses
- Leather and cotton gloves
- First aid kit, survival kit, GPS and mobile phone
- Good-operating shotgun and backup shotgun in a Gun Rap case to keep the guns dry
- Federal BBB shells in a waterproof shell box
- Gun cleaning kit and supplies, necessary license and stamps
- Dependable 4x4 truck and necessary trailer
- Tow chain and jumper cables
- Tool box/tools
- Thermos, coolers, alarm clock and shaving kit

30 dozen silhouettes will be light and will work for these clever snow geese. Outlaw is the best silhouette to purchase.

Some of the items mentioned might need explaining:

1. Plastic sleds. Great for pulling your gear out onto your field, and also great to lay in especially when it is wet and muddy.

2. Hole puncher. The ground will be frozen and will break stakes for your silhouettes and North Winds. You will definitely need this puncher on this late season trip!

3. White sheets. Great for snow. These can be used to cover up blinds and other equipment that sticks out on a snowy field.

4. White hats, face masks and coveralls. Think snow!

5. License and stamps. Pay attention here! You might not need a new Federal stamp; check your stamps from the earlier season for expiration dates.

6. Waterproof shell box. You will encounter mud and wet conditions. Take care of your shells and avoid a misfire.

Goose hunting involves a lot of packing, a lot of hard work, and a lot of expense to go after a little white bird that might weigh 5 pounds. You have to be a little bit crazy to be a goose hunter!

D. How To Hunt Late Season Snow Geese.

This late season goose hunt might be an adventure for you. If you stay with the basics and display some patience, you could make it happen. You have to hunt until dark because if the wind is calm or blowing from the south, there will be geese migrating into your area late in the afternoon. Don't expect the geese to hang around your area long. They are going to an area where there are lots of geese, water and safety. You have to be an opportunist and get them quick. Staying in the blind is one suggestion I might offer. You won't kill geese in your motel room or a bar. It has never happened before! If the weather turns extremely cold, the geese could migrate south, especially if their roost freezes over. That could interrupt your hunting for 4 to 7 days. The weather will change quickly and will surprise you.

How to hunt depends on the type of place you get to hunt on. Secure a spot near water for openers. The geese will be desperate to find water and get a drink.

Obtaining permission to hunt a corn field with standing water or water nearby is essential. The geese will be coming in tired, hungry and thirsty and you have to have what they want. If the geese are

Put out some North Wind windsocks and use an Eliminator blind. Pay attention to the weather also.

migrating in and out, you might want to keep the same field all week, if it is a good field.

Concealment is your most important factor. You have to be concealed. You don't want a dog with and you need a low-profile blind such as my Eliminators. If you don't have one of those, use natural cover to hide in or gather corn stalks or weeds and cover up. Don't lay in the decoy spread. Be 40 yards downwind from the decoys. Don't use a bale or stand-up blind. Those won't work hunting against these clever geese and strong winds.

Here is what I would do under these different situations:

Wind is from the north or northwest. Don't expect any migration of geese. For decoys, try 288 North Wind windsocks only. Spread them out three feet apart. You don't need a kite or hovering because there is too much wind. Stay in your blinds because you don't know what might be moving around.

Wind is strong from the south. Expect a migration of geese after 11am. Try 144 North Wind windsocks only and spread them out three feet apart. Be alert in the afternoon because the geese will be migrating 1,000 yards up. You will hear them before you will see them.

Snow and wind combined. Use 120 silhouettes and 72 North Wind windsocks only. Use the low-profile silhouettes only because of the windy conditions. Make sure you push your windsocks deep to prevent them from blowing over. Use a hole puncher if necessary. For concealment: Watch the geese if they are flying low. You might get in a fence row or tree line and catch them coming in low at your decoys.

Normal conditions: Expect some migration of geese. If you have windless conditions, use 360 silhouettes and spread them out. Don't use any kites, windsocks or hovering decoys if you are hunting without wind.

SUMMARY: Hang in there and hope the wind blows from the south. If it does, you will have some great Spring weather and some good hunting. You should get some migrating geese. If the weather turns ugly, expect the worst. GOOD LUCK TO YOU!

The author with some nice birds taken during the late snow goose season in Nebraska (early 1998).

Advice About!

A. WEATHER.

This is something that the average goose hunter doesn't think about or concentrate enough on. The odds against a goose hunter getting a goose are long. When the weather changes and gets nasty, the odds change. They get even or in favor of goose hunters. That is when you have to react and move quickly. This is "pay back time" and it doesn't last very long.

Birds and animals have a sixth sense about the weather. When a low pressure system is moving in and the barometric pressure is dropping, they feel this and become alerted. They might go into a feeding frenzy and that is when they can be had if you strike quickly. The geese will feed close to roads, fly low and slow, and do other dumb things. Feeding will be more important to them and you have to take advantage of this.

A massive low pressure system moved through the midwest on November 8, 1998 and it set records in some areas. The geese felt it and were on the move. Some great hunts were recorded during this time because some alert goose hunters capitalized on the weather. The low pressure and high winds threw the geese a curve and knocked them off balance. The daily limit of snow geese is 20 in North Dakota, and Gage Dargan from Fargo and Scott Butz from Argusville, North Dakota got their limits on November 9, 1998. The geese were desperate to feed and these two hunters were in fields where the geese just kept coming and coming. They took advantage of the snow geese, as you can see in the picture on the facing page.

I have been in the same situations where my companions and I killed 40 to 50 geese because the weather threw the birds off their normal patterns,

A 20-snow-goose limit was taken by Gage Dargan from Fargo, North Dakota on November 9, 1998 while hunting in poor weather after a low-pressure system moved through. (A few of the geese in this photo belong to other hunting companions.)

and we were able to take advantage of that fact. During that same low-pressure system that Gage and Scott enjoyed, the west winds blew and the snow geese were pushed hundreds of miles east. Geese ended up on the ground at Cedar Rapids, Iowa instead of De Soto National Wildlife Refuge near Blair, Nebraska. 500,000 of them could not stay on course and were forced to stop at Cedar Rapids, stay two days and then fly west to De Soto. Windom, Minnesota had 15,000 white geese as visitors for a couple weeks; these birds originally intended to stop at Sloan, Iowa. When this sort of unusual weather condition happens, you'll get a goose for dinner if you strike quickly.

Weather systems will cause fog, rain, snow and low clouds. Let me tell you how I would react.

• **Fog.** Mark your fields for the next day with GPS

The weather is unpredictable and you have to be ready to make changes when it changes. Pray for a fog such as this.

or reflector tape. Put out your largest decoys and give yourself two extra hours to find your way in the fog.

- **Rain.** Poor vision is associated with rain so you should mark your fields with GPS or reflector tape. If there is also wind, put out 144 North Wind windsocks only. If there isn't any wind, put out Outlaw silhouettes or Flambeau shells. Put on a rain suit and bring extra outfits, gloves, hat and boots, and get ready for a miserable hunting day.
- **Snow.** Mark your fields with GPS or reflector tape and set out for your field two hours early in the morning. Put out your largest decoys and bring along a brush to sweep snow off the decoys as it accumulates. Dress warmly and bring stocking hats, extra gloves and extra boots.
- **Clouds.** Cloudy weather helps a goose hunter, especially if the clouds are dark and low. Put out your largest decoys, and some North Wind wind-socks if there is wind. A Jackite will also work if there's wind; use a pole and pole holder.

Stay in touch with any changes in the weather, and try to catch a forecast on the radio if you can.

Some remote areas in Canada don't offer much in this regard. Be alert, especially if it becomes windy. My favorite statement is:

No wind, no geese; more wind, more geese!

This statement is right on. Poor weather conditions help the goose hunter and also makes him miserable. Keep your hat on and GOOD LUCK!

B. CONCEALMENT.

I stumbled around for years and ignored concealment. I never realized how well a goose can see. I have killed over 10,000 geese shooting them alone or with someone else and probably could have killed another 5,000 if I had figured out the art of concealment earlier in my goose-hunting career. I am not bragging, because I have hunted them for 33 years and thousands of hours. I know now that I have

Don't take concealment for granted. Get a low-profile blind, or cover up 40 yards downwind from the decoys using straw, cornstalks or weeds. Look at Dennis Hunt and his Eliminator blind.

committed a lot of sins against concealment. These cardinal sins were:

1. I had a dog out on the field with me.

2. I laid within the decoy spread, either wearing white or camouflage (but I shouldn't have been there in the first place).

3. I never wore a face mask.

4. I built a blind within the decoy spread.

5. My hunting companions and I moved too much.

6. My hunting companions smoked in the blind.

7. I never built or purchased a low-profile blind.

So now I offer this prayer:

"Dear Goose God—
Forgive me for I knew not
what I was doing. I am older and wiser
and won't let it happen again.
--Dennis Hunt"

This sums up the mistakes a goose hunter can make. He doesn't realize how important **concealment** is. Compare a goose hunter to a goose and this is what you have (remember, the goose is in the air):

	GOOSE HUNTER	GOOSE
VISIBILITY (clear weather with unlimited visibility, flat land)	3 miles	25 miles
HEARING (calm conditions)	20 yards	3 miles

I started out goose hunting the same way other young goose hunters start out. I used a firing line, I used ambush tactics and I hid in the fence lines. I graduated up to using field decoys, but then committed all those sins against **concealment.** Look at

If you don't have a low-profile blind, you can save some money by using burlap bags and straw. Throw it over your pretty face and it will work. Stay 40 yards downwind of the decoy spread.

the sins again and see how many you commit or have committed while goose hunting.

Things that can HELP you:

1. Use straw or corn stalks to cover up with.
2. Cover up with white sheets, camouflage or burlap sacks.
3. Use a back rest for comfort, and cover up with straw.
4. Find natural cover, i.e. a farm implement, dried-up swamp, low spots in the field, ditch, weed patches or a rock pile.
5. Dig a pit.

Things that can HURT you:

1. Lying within the decoy spread.
2. Having a dog with you.
3. More than four hunters in the field.
4. Using camouflage that doesn't blend in with the field.

You want to be concealed so well that these turkeys would walk right past you. If this happens to you, you've passed the concealment test.

5. Not being properly camouflaged, or using camouflage that shines.
6. Not playing the wind and lying in the wrong spot.
7. Using the wrong kind of blind:
    a. Gooseview Lodge: It is dangerous because you can't get out of it.
    b. Pop-Up: It is too high; it should be lower-profile.
    c. Gooseview Bale Blind: It can be dangerous unless it is staked down. It shakes, rattles and rolls in the wind. It might be an accident waiting to happen. Materials are too bright as well; ducks and geese flare off it.
    d. Goose chair: This utilizes the lying-within-the-decoys scenario and is bad for that reason.

I have tried and used the above products many times. I am sorry if I offended any purchaser or manufacturer, but this is my humble opinion and my intent is to help goose hunters.

The summary is, don't take **concealment** for granted! This is your most important factor in harvesting a goose.

C. DECOYS AND DECOY SPREADS.

In my opinion, field hunting by using goose decoys is an exciting challenge. It allows the goose hunter to match wits with the goose.

Geese are attracted to decoys like metal to a magnet. The decoys should represent geese that are feeding. Since geese are usually hungry, they fly toward the decoys and try to convince themselves that the decoys are live geese and the field safe to land in. Instinct will prevail if the decoys can't convince the geese, and they will flare off the field and fly away.

When matching wits with a goose, it is to your advantage to know how long the geese have been in your hunting area. Here are factors to consider:

1. If they just migrated in, they don't know your field or decoys yet.
2. If they have been in your hunting area seven days, they have already seen you, your field and your decoys.
3. If they have been in your hunting area 14 days or more, they know everything about you, your field and your decoys.

Geese live by a super memory. You won't get a chance to try to shoot at the same flock of geese that came over yesterday and looked at your spread of decoys; it won't happen again. Why should it? These geese don't want to die and they will avoid you and your field of decoys.

Use your imagination and try different strategies on the geese. Use different formations of decoys. I use: horseshoe, diamond, straight lines and an X. Try a different one every day until you trigger the geese and get them in close. You have to be creative and try some of the following:

- Use a kite decoy.
- Use different styles of decoys.

- Use less or more decoys.
- Use one "family" of six decoys.
- Use more movement decoys.
- Try not calling, or try a call with a different pitch.
- Try flagging or not flagging.

I am trying to trigger the geese by using something different every day. My best days have been:

1. Using 24 or fewer Canada decoys on Canada geese.

2. Using 72 or less snow goose decoys on snows.

REMEMBER. You are matching wits with old geese that have seen and heard it all. They don't want to die, and they have great memories.

Your selection of quality goose hunting equipment is very important to your success in killing a goose. You need the right equipment to get the job done. You can't afford to make mistakes, because mistakes cost money and will cause you frustrations out on the goose hunting fields.

Getting started will cost you and your hunting team of four about $1,000.00 apiece to get a good arsenal of equipment that will get the job done. Add $100.00 each per year thereafter and you will always be competitive. BEWARE. When making each purchase, get a second opinion. There is a lot of junk out there and some of the manufacturers selling this equipment used to sell cars. TRUST ME! I purchased all of this junk because I am an impulse buyer and a "goose hunting nut." If you ever want an opinion on goose hunting equipment, call, fax or write me at:

Dennis Hunt
1265 Loring Avenue #205
Detroit Lakes, MN 56501
Fax and phone: 218-847-5147

Aren't these Higdon and Clinton decoys realistic? They work super.

You have read my list of what is needed in the previous chapters. We will not go over my preferences of trucks, trailers, guns, clothing or personal items. I will give you an opinion and list of quality goose hunting equipment to purchase. I hope I don't offend any purchaser or manufacturer. I am just trying to help the goose hunter get started and get to a higher level of ability. I have tried it all and am qualified to tell it like it is.

STILL DECOYS:
- <u>Full-bodies with feet</u>: This is a great decoy. Higdon and Clinton have the most realistic.
- <u>Shells</u>: This decoy is almost obsolete! Geese know what these decoys are because they've seen them for 100 years and the decoys don't move.
- <u>Silhouettes</u>: Outlaw is the pioneer of this decoy and they make the best. There are a lot of imitators out there and a lot of junk sold. It only costs a little more to go first class.

Another nice-looking decoy spread. If your decoy spread looks alive, with decoys moving in the breeze, you will get more geese to visit.

MOVEMENT DECOYS:

- <u>Full-body</u>: The Higdon system with the soft head uses a cam to create movement, and there is no comparison. This system is a little more money and trouble, but I have killed a lot of geese with it.
- <u>Windsocks</u>: North Wind invented the greatest decoy of all time 20 years ago, and this decoy has helped goose hunters harvest more geese than any other. I have harvested over 10,000 using this decoy; it really works!
- <u>Texas rag</u>: This economical decoy sells for 25 cents. Should I say more? It is plastic and I have seen them shine on occasion, so be careful.
- <u>North Wind hovering</u>: This is a new style for North Wind; see the picture below. This decoy is ten times more effective than the goose magnet, and it is made in the U.S.A. Trust me! I used the goose magnet for 9 years, and I know.
- <u>Goose magnet</u>: I have had flares off the wings and heads of these decoys. The old style was much

Here is a close-up view of some great-looking Outlaw silhouette decoys. They really fool the geese, and are lightweight to carry.

better. I have been a union man, and I don't like to buy decoys that are made in China as these are.

KITE DECOYS:

- Jackite: This company is the inventor and pioneer of all quality kites. There were other kites but Jackite makes quality.
- Outlaw: They went to school on Jackite and came up with a good kite and worthy of a look.
- Killer Kite: I call this kite "the spinner.". This kite has killed me many times. I had flocks of geese come in and this kite would spin to the ground, the geese would fly away and I would swear.
- Farm Form: A plastic kite with a short life span.

FLOATER DECOYS:

- Higdon has no comparison. Their floater can be worked off a line that creates movement of the head. It is a winner!

D. OTHER EQUIPMENT.
BLINDS:

- <u>Final Approach Eliminator</u>: There is no comparison! This blind is what a blind is supposed to do—give you some comfort and hide you from the geese. This blind does that and does it well. I had a great goose hunting season against snow geese and I have told you how wary this goose is. It weighs just 12 pounds!

Two Eliminator blinds in a Manitoba barley field. Does it get any better than this?

- <u>Gooseview Lodge</u>: This blind is dangerous! I had to pull too many of my hunting companions out of this blind. Once you get in, you can't get out without help. An accident waiting to happen, especially if you are in that blind with a gun.
- <u>Gooseview Bale Blind</u>: Another accident waiting to happen. You cannot use this blind in the wind without staking it down on all four sides. I have seen it blown down hills by the wind on

The Gooseview Bale Blind has been a nightmare for me. Everything that should have gone right has gone wrong. It looks good, but I would not recommend it. I did recommend it to 50 goose hunters, and they are mad at me after trying this phony piece of straw.

many occasions with hunters, guns, stools, coffee etc. falling out of the blind. I have used this blind many times and it shakes, rattles and rolls in the wind. The material on the sides and flaps shines and flares the ducks and geese. TRUST ME! I bought this blind with confidence and was disappointed.

- Pop-Up Blind: This blind is too high-profile.

BOOTS:
- Sorel: I have had many pairs of boots in 33 years of goose hunting and Sorel makes a great boot. I have tried them all!

SHELLS:
- Federal Ammunition: I have used Federal for 33 years, fired over 50,500 rounds (200 cases), and never had a mis-fire. I attribute that to:
  1. Cleaning my gun after each hunting outing.
  2. Keeping my shells warm and dry while out in the field.
  3. Using Federal Shells.

I hope this section on equipment will assist you. I have tried it all and have been disappointed over the years and very satisfied as well. *The statements are my personal opinions. No one has paid me to make any statements for or against any manufacturers.*

Get your shotgun up quickly, lead the geese and always follow through. If you follow the fundamentals, you can enjoy goose hunting success like Dennis Hunt.

E. SHOOTING.

Anyone can shoot a shotgun but not everyone can hit their targets. Good shooting is a mental game. If you have confidence in your gun and shells and are relaxed, you will shoot well. If you are goose hunting and you get off to a late start in the morning, can't find the correct field and you are hunting with three other jerks, you won't hit a bull in the rear end with a hand full of rice. It is all confidence!

I have always shot well. I have used a Winchester Model 50, 12-gauge automatic that shoots 2¾-inch shells. I also use a 10-gauge Ithaca that shoots 3½-inch shells. I use Federal BBB for geese. I have used the Winchester for 33 years and the Ithaca for 20 years. I don't believe in trading guns if you are shooting well. Why should you? I was in the golf business for 30 years and would have some golfers come in four times a year and trade in their clubs. They never took a lesson nor would they blame themselves. It was always, "the clubs."

A veteran hunter told me 30 years ago, "You can never lead a goose far enough." That was good advice! By the time the last piece of steel leaves the hull of your shell and travels 50 yards to a goose flying 55 or more miles per hour, it is a long time. By shooting ahead of the goose, you have a chance. Shooting behind the goose will give you no chance.

Getting your shotgun up quickly, leading the goose, and following through is the advice I am going to give you. I never practice at the range because I am always fishing. I hunt 6 months a year and never seem to lose my shooting ability.

Summary

Getting to be a very good goose hunter will take many years of hunting. You go from one level to another as you will encounter difficult situations that will take "good judgement" and as you master that situation, you will move up to another level. You will be using common sense and sticking to the basics as you go along. Your game plans will get better and will eliminate the mistakes you used to make. Your harvests will increase and hunting will be a lot more fun with less frustrations. Everything will fall in place as you gather some confidence. Always be humble and try to learn something about goose hunting every day. Never get over-confident because that could result in an accident. Never under-estimate the word CONCEALMENT. You will agree with me after you get experience, that this is the most important factor in harvesting a goose.

I am going to leave you with three recipes from goose hunting friends. I hope you enjoy them. I hope to run into you at a sports show or sporting goods store as I give a goose hunting seminar. If not, I hope to see you out in a goose hunting field as you are picking up your limit of geese. Feel free to call me, fax me or write me if you want to talk goose hunting, order a book or video or have a goose hunting question for me.

Dennis Hunt
1265 Loring Ave. #205
Detroit Lakes, MN 56501
Fax and Phone: 218-847-5147

Recipes

Goose Shore Lunch
by Gary Roach, Mr. Walleye
Presented by Scott Hanson, Buffalo, MN

Cut goose breast into thin strips or small chunks. Add a small portion of onions and mushrooms. Mix in a ziplock bag with Gary Roach's Original Shore Lunch mix. Place coated meat pieces in a hot frying pan with hot cooking oil. Do not overcook. Serve on a bed of rice.
    Serves 2.

Goose Gordie
by Gordon Steinwig, Brooklyn Park, MN

- Cut goose in small pieces.
- Place meat in a marinade of your choice.
- Add Worcestershire sauce, granulated garlic and onion powder, and cracked pepper to the blend.
- Place in a ziplock bag for 24 hours.
- Heat oil until hot in a non-stick pan: gradually add meat to hot oil, and cook until meat is browned.
- Boil raw wild rice for 20 minutes, then add Uncle Ben's original rice mix and spice package to boiling rice as directed. Add butter to the rice as it cooks.
- Serve meat on top of rice.
  Serves 2.

Goose Girard
by Girard Faith, Audubon, MN

6 goose breasts, skinned
1½ tablespoons flour, baked until browned
1½ tablespoons butter
1 sliced onion
1 cup water
1 cube chicken bouillon
6 pieces of toast

Bake goose at 500°F until goose is medium rare, about 15 minutes. While baking goose, make the roux in a saucepan: melt butter over medium heat, then add the onion rings and cook until the are limp. Remove the onion rings and stir the flour into the butter in the saucepan. Remove the saucepan from the heat. Boil the water, then add the chicken bouillon cube and stir until dissolved. Add the chicken broth to the roux in the saucepan and mix well. Heat the mixture over medium heat, stirring constantly, until it gets glossy; it will not form a gravy.

Take goose out of oven and slice ⅛ inch thin. Put the slices on the toast. Pour desired amount of sauce over the goose.

Serves 2 or 3.

Previous Books by Dennis Hunt

Dennis Hunt is the author of three previous books on goose hunting: *The Science of Snow Goose Hunting, Goose Hunting: Improving Your Skills, Out-Finessing The Geese* and *The Goose Hunter: The Ultimate Goose Hunting Season.* They are available at selected sporting-goods stores and bookstores, and can also be purchased directly from Dennis Hunt for $19.95 each (U.S. postage included). Send a check or Visa card number to Dennis Hunt at the address listed below.

Dennis Hunt also has produced a beautiful color video entitled "The Science of Goose Hunting: Improving Your Skills," which is available for $19.95.

Seminars

Dennis Hunt gives goose-hunting seminars at many sports shows across the country. Check the listings at your next local sports show; if Dennis is not one of the featured speakers, let the show management know you'd like to see him at a seminar!

Dennis Hunt
1265 Loring Ave. #205
Detroit Lakes, MN 56501
Fax and Phone: 218-847-5147

3489